The Position of Your Heart
and The Healing of a Nation

By
Shelly J. Bishop

A 40 Day Journey of the Heart

Acknowledgments
Cover design by Vicky Weeks, Graphic by artist Wanda
Ide-Wilburn.

Thank You
A sincere and heartfelt thank you to those leaders, worshippers,
and firebrands whom I have had the privilege to run with and
have helped me along my journey. Thank you for being who God
created you to be. I pray that God pours out abundantly on you!
Overflowing! You have sown much into many and
will reap bountifully!
Tina Baker, Jacquie Tyre, Clay Nash, Dutch Sheets, Jim and Joan
Rawlins, Bill Easter, Lynda and Joe Diandio, Glenna Burkett, Cathy
Dickenson, Daphne Swilling, Doug Snead,
Sue Gordon, Randy Webb, Sylvia Gast, Saundra Corner, Eddie
James, Darla Patterson, Mark and Sandie Burger, Bob Luczynski,
Bob and June Myers, Gloria Bordeaux
and all the other
worshipping warriors who have released their sounds into this
region, shifted atmospheres, scattered enemies and
stayed the course!
You, my friend, have made a difference!
Thank you

Dedication

I dedicate this book to all those hungry lovers of God who are seeking more of God in all areas of their lives. May God encounter you in a fresh new way that changes your life forever. May God Mark you for revival and may you become a living flame of fire, determined to burn for Him and catch others ablaze as you go.

A Special thank you also to my mom whose love and support were always there for me. She taught us well and always wanted the best for all of us. She was the glue that held us together.
I love you, Mom.

This book is also for my 4 daughters, my 3 grandsons and my husband who may not have always understood me but whom I have always loved beyond measure. I pray that you all find the God of Love and God of Fire that I have known and fall in love with Him, as I have. Make it your life purpose.

Thank you also to all the worshipping warriors that I have had the privilege and honor to share this journey with. Stand strong until the end. Father has placed you here for such a time as this and there's no turning back.
Arise Warrior Bride! It's time to release your ROAR!
Tell them we're coming and heaven's coming with us!

Table of Contents

Day   Title

1. *The God Who Answers by Fire*
2. *Your Season of Preparation*
3. *Arise My Warrior Bride*
4. *Time to Come Out of the Cave*
5. *Child of God, There is Hope*
6. *The Characteristics of God's True Army*
7. *Overcoming Fear and Walking in Power and Authority*
8. *Offense Will Teach or Kill - You Choose*
9. *Praise Your Way Through the Sufferings*
10. *The Power of the Word*
11. *Go to Your Room*
12. *The Transforming Power of God*
13. *Rise Up Child of God, You Are Not a Slave but a Son*
14. *Competition Kills*
15. *God's Perfect Gift*
16. *Jesus' Commission was Simple-Come and Then Go*
17. *Be Holy You Vessel of Honor*
18. *What Are You Sowing?*
19. *Conquer or Be Conquered*
20. *The Battle is Still Over Who You Will Worship*
21. *Barrenness Can Birth Greatness*
22. *The Power of His Love*
23. *Make the Devil Pay*
24. *Rend the Heavens*
25. *You Have Great Purpose*
26. *Life on the Threshing Floor*

27. A Circumcised Heart

28. A False Gospel of Self

29. The Cross Cries Love

30. Your Season of Job

31. Kicking Against the Goads

32. Giants Will Fall

33. Anger is a Destroyer

34. Destination Glory

35. Who Will Rule Your Region?

36. David's Greatest Accomplishment

37. Throwing Spears or Dodging Spears

38. The Freedom is in the Forgiveness

39. What I've Learned

40. Tell Them We're Coming

Author's Note

About

Shelly J. Bishop is the mother of 4 beautiful daughters and has 3 handsome grandsons. She has been married for 31 years. She is the founder and leader of The House of the Living God in Mineral Bluff Ga. and CityGate Freedom Place, Kingdom Resource Center in McCaysville Ga. where she trains and equips people to discover their identity in Christ, walk out their calling and fulfill their God-given destiny.

She has a passion to see people healed, set free, delivered and equipped and activated in their calling. She is an Apostolic leader and teacher and is also a Life Keys Recovery Facilitator and the Director of The House of the Living God Healing Room. She is commissioned by NEI (Network Ekklesia International).

Purpose

This book was birthed out of a deep passion to see people healed, set free, delivered and walking out the call of God on their life as they become the person that God created them to be. I started writing a weekly column in the local paper several years ago for that very purpose. The newspaper was called "The Fannin Sentinel." The editor was very gracious and enjoyed my writings and allowed me to continue to write for several years until Covid forced them to close. That's when God began to nudge me to finish the book I had begun several years earlier. I argued with Him, of course, saying nobody would want to read a book like that. But as an obedient lover of God, when Holy Spirit directs, you must obey. This book is written in obedience to My Heavenly

Father and I pray that He puts it in the hands of those that He wants to read it and I pray that it touches hearts and leads people closer to God.

It's not fancy, it's not perfect. But it's mine. You may even find some errors. But that's OK. It just proves that God can use anybody who is obedient and surrendered to Him. My reward is for My Father to say, "Well done, My Child." It is my prayer that as you read this book that you find yourself falling in love with God and Jesus all over again. I pray that it encourages you to press on and finish your race and finish strong. May your latter days be greater than your former and may you step out and become all that God has created you to be. May you rise up as the mighty warrior that God created you to be and wreak havoc on the kingdom of darkness.

Challenge
I challenge you to rise up as a warrior and soldier in the Army of God and join in with me as we decree: **America is one Nation Under God! God Bless America! Tell the enemy we're coming and Heaven's coming with us!**

The Position of Your Heart and The Healing of a Nation

Introduction

When God first started speaking to me about "The Position of My Heart", I thought, " Oh wait God, don't you mean the condition of my heart? You know my heart, Lord." But He quickly corrected me and said, "No, I'm looking at the **position** of your heart, not the condition." I gently asked Him, "Lord, what position do you want my heart to be in?" He softly and gently replied, "I want your heart positioned in My hands, so I can mold it, heal it, shape it, into what I want it to be. "

My question to you today is, "What is the position of your heart?" God is looking at the position of our hearts. Life can be hard. We all go through trials, tribulations, heartaches and heartbreaks that leave wounds and scars as big as Texas in our hearts. Even when we are trying our best to do what's right, we get wounded along the way. However, we must learn to find God's perfect grace for our lives or we will find ourselves walking in fear, offense, unforgiveness, hatred, jealousy, bitterness, rejection and numerous other heart issues. God is looking at your heart today. He wants to take it in His hands and heal those battle scars for you and set you free from the brokenness that you are carrying so you can fulfill your destiny.

There's an old saying that still rings true today: It says, "Hurt people, hurt people." Sometimes we get hurt by the world, our family, society and sometimes even by the church. Either way, it's painful. But thank God we serve a God who specializes in restoration, regeneration and reconciliation. He's the master at healing the brokenhearted and setting the captives free. That's one reason why He came. (Luke 4:18 - My life verse too)

When we come to God with a humble heart and ask Him to heal us, He hears us and comes to our rescue. Healing can be painful but it's well worth the pain to get you to your purpose. John 16:21 relates it to a woman who is in labor, giving birth to her promise. As a mother of 4 beautiful girls, I know the pain of childbirth. But as soon as you hold that baby in your arms, the pain subsides and you soon forget the process. There will always be pain on the path to your promise. There are trials, tribulations, tragedies and deep struggles that we must go through to reach our destiny.

God is a master at turning your pain into purpose. He will turn your test into a testimony and your mess into a message. When you place your heart in His hands, He will reach inside and find those broken places that have held you hostage and kept you from fulfilling your purpose. He will bring healing and wholeness and give you joy and peace beyond measure, but you have to humbly allow Him access to those sensitive places.

Psalms 51:10-11 (AMP) says, "Create in me a clean heart, O God, And renew a right and steadfast spirit within me. Do not cast me away from Your presence And do not take Your Holy Spirit from me."

Turn your heart toward God today, submit and surrender to Him and allow Him to heal you of all the wounds you have accumulated in life. He came to set you free and heal you of all that brings you sorrow and distress. He came that you would have abundant life! He loves you and He's waiting with outstretched arms toward you. When you do, you will find peace and your life will never be the same.

I believe that as the people get healed individually that the nation will be turned back to God and the land (or nation) will be healed. As the church, we have stood on the verse 2 Chr 7:14; Praying it and Decreeing it. Now it's time to "live it." God is calling **His people** to humble themselves, repent and pray and seek His face. He's NOT calling the masses or the multitudes or the world. He's calling His People. That's me and you. It is my prayer that we each do our part and allow God to bring total healing to all parts of our hearts and let it spread to others.

2Ch 7:14 (ESV) If my people who are called by my name humble themselves, and pray and seek my face and turn from their wicked ways, then I will hear from heaven and will forgive their sin and heal their land.

Give it a try. Close your eyes, lift up your hands toward heaven and say, "Father God, I surrender my heart to you. I place it in your hands to do with it whatsoever you desire. It is yours. Bring healing to every broken place and make me whole and then Lord, as I get healed, let it go out from here and bring healing to others and to our nation. Let it start with me."

Day 1
The God Who Answers By Fire

When God wants to put His mark or His brand on someone or some place or some thing He uses fire. You, my friend, have been marked by the Fire of God!

1Ki 18:24 (ESV) And you call upon the name of your god, and I will call upon the name of the LORD, and the God who answers by fire, he is God." And all the people answered, "It is well spoken."

Every day you just need to lay yourself on God's altar and ask Him to burn up everything that is within you that is not of Him and to take anything that is separating you from Him. Lying prostrate on the floor before God symbolizes submission and humility. It is at the altar that He will alter you.

Our God is an all-consuming flame and He wants us to rebuild the altar of sacrifice, lay ourselves upon it, and become that living sacrifice for Him. He wants to baptize us with fresh fire. As we surrender our hearts and lives to God, He will come into our hearts in a real and powerful way and we will be turned into a different person; the person that He created us to be all along, not who the world says we are or even who we say we are, but who Heaven says we are.

Hebrews 12:28-29 (NLT) Since we are receiving a Kingdom that is unshakable, let us be thankful and please God by worshiping him with holy fear and awe. For our God is a devouring (consuming) fire.

As we go through the fire and the testings, it is here that we find out what we are really made of. When the pressure is applied, what's inside will come out. In this war that we are in, Satan is raging and out to destroy and deceive all of those that he can reach. Don't be a casualty and don't be deceived. You are on one side or the other, whether you want to be or not. There is no middle ground. You cannot remain neutral in a time of war. Fence straddlers become casualties in wartime. When the people of God are complacent and sit by silently, it strengthens the hand of the enemy. Don't get caught aiding and abetting the enemy. Silence speaks loud in a time of war. It is not time to be silent. It's time for the church to roar!

God comes as a refining fire to purify and strengthen us. He uses warfare to strengthen us and get us to the place where He wants us to be. God's consuming fire will burn away the things inside you that are not of Him, such as fear, hate, unforgiveness, bitterness, rejection, impatience and doubt. We all are hanging on to some things that are not of God that we need to get rid of. Lay it all on the altar right now. Go ahead. I'm waiting. Symbolically just reach inside your heart and grab those things that are holding you hostage and lay them at the altar.

Galatians 5 tells us the fruits of the Spirit are love, joy, peace, patience, kindness, goodness, faithfulness, gentleness and self-control. This is what should make up the character of the children of God. Anything outside of that is not of God. God wants us to reflect Him and the only way to do that is to surrender ourselves to Him and allow Him to transform us into His image.

Through the trials and the tests and the surrender and submission, our character is formed. We learn to withstand every battle. We learn compassion for others and how to stand strong and we develop a tenacity to stand and a perseverance to push through hard times and not give up. We learn to recognize the enemy and his tricks and tactics. So God takes the very thing that Satan uses to try and destroy you (warfare) and He turns it around and uses it to strengthen you. (warfare) Isn't God amazing!

Like metal forged in a fire; It's hammered, pounded, stretched, repeatedly and then it's plunged back into the fire again and again. The fire gives it power and flexibility and the repeated blows give it strength. It burns away the dross and all the impurities and what remains is pure and holy. *The toughest and finest steel is forged in the hottest fire and you will be too.*

Deu 4:24 (KJV) For the LORD thy God is a consuming fire, even a jealous God.

When you go through the fire, it's the adversities, the struggles and the trials of life, that form you into His image. Like with the metal, the impurities are brought to the surface, cast out or burned up and what remains is strong, resolute and pure. Those impurities intensify the fire, like wood or stubble would intensify a fire in the natural. But they also cause a separation from God. God is looking for vessels that He can empty out, purify and fill with His Spirit and His goodness.

Forging isn't comfortable. First, you start off with scrap metal that is normally worthless and not much good for anything if left in that state. But as you take it through the forging process, you will see it transformed into what is called the world's most useful structural material; hardened carbon steel. Can you see the correlation? It's the same analogy as the lump of clay that winds up in the potter's hands and becomes a beautiful vessel, useful to the master for every good work. (2 Tim 2:21)

In forming the metal, there's pounding and stretching and then you plunge the metal in oil or water to harden it. If that process works and is done correctly a file will not leave a mark or scar on it. Hammering the steel refines the grain structure of the metal, giving it strength and superiority. In the spirit realm, the oil and water represent the Holy Spirit; this plunging causes a humbling in your spirit; A total dependence on the forger, which is your Father in Heaven. Allow God to be your forger and plunge you into the fire again and again until He decides that you are ready. Allow Him to mold you into what He created you to be all along. Surrender yourself fully to Him, so that you don't strengthen the hand of the enemy and become a pawn in Satan's evil plan to kill, steal and destroy.

Rev 3:18 (ESV) I counsel you to buy from me gold refined by fire, so that you may be rich, and white garments so that you may clothe yourself and the shame of your nakedness may not be seen, and salve to anoint your eyes, so that you may see.

Our God is a God of Love and a God of Fire. He loves us so much that He refuses to allow us to stay in the same condition that He found us in, like the worthless metal. It's His Love that releases His

Fire. God likes Fire. The word "Love" appears in the Bible 311 times, yet the word "Fire " appears in the Bible 549 times. (KJV) He knows exactly what each person needs. Sometimes He woos His children into His arms and sometimes He snatches them out of the fire. It takes both His Love and His Fire. Allow both to come to your heart, as God chooses, as He has the divine order of healing and restoration for you.

Jud 1:22-23 (TPT) Keep being compassionate to those who still have doubts, and snatch others out of the fire to save them. Be merciful over and over to them, but always couple your mercy with the fear of God. Be extremely careful to keep yourselves free from the pollutions of the flesh.

When you have been in the fire of God; when you have felt His fiery presence; when you have seen the fire in His eyes; You will be marked for life. Nothing else will ever satisfy you. You will never again be satisfied with the lukewarm status quo of "normal" church. You will develop such a deep hunger for the things of God and His presence that you will never look at church the same way. You, like David, will seek out a cave if need be just to be in His presence.

Are you there yet? Congratulations. You, my friend, have been marked by the Fire of God. You are turning back to your first love. Go ahead. It's OK. God never wanted you to leave from there anyway.

It is my prayer that you develop a deep love and hunger for God like you have never experienced before. May the Holy Spirit baptize you with fresh fire as He changes you from the inside out.

I see you as a burning one! Expect radical changes to take place in your life as you embrace the Fire of God.

Day 2
Your Season of Preparation

Psalm 105:19 (NLT) Until the time came to fulfill his dreams, the Lord tested Joseph's character.

Everything God does is in order and for a specific purpose. He doesn't waste anything. When He puts a dream in your heart, you will go through testing before the dream comes to pass and the greater the dream, the greater the test.

God uses the tests to prove our character in order to make sure we don't waste the dream. He knows when He gives us the dream that we aren't ready to handle the fulfillment of it. However, in all His wisdom, He places it in our hearts and then He starts the process of purging and testing to prepare us to carry the dream. He does whatever He needs to do to help us become the person who will properly steward the dream.

Psalms 139:23-24 (NLT) Search me, O God, and know my heart; test me and know my anxious thoughts. Point out anything in me that offends you, and lead me along the path of everlasting life.

If God has given you a dream, and you want to fulfill it, then be prepared to be tested. There is no way around it. If you want to fulfill the dream, you must pass the test. He must first prepare your heart to carry His dream. (Yes it's His dream-He just chose to use you to bring it to pass) It will take some perseverance to make it happen but it will be worth it. It takes time. Don't rush it.

19

The preparation season always seems to move slow. The nine months before the birthing seems SLOW. The time between the planting and the harvest seems SLOW.

At the time of his dream, Joseph was a young 17-year-old prideful tattletale. His own brothers despised him. They sold him as a slave which meant that he would always be a slave and his children would always be slaves, under normal conditions. Then falsely accused, he was thrown in the dungeon with no hope of escape. In the natural, It looked as though his dream was only a dream and it would never be fulfilled. But God, as always, had a plan.

Joseph's prison time seemed SLOW. It was nearly 14 years between his dream and the time he left prison to become second in command of Egypt. It was about 10 more years before his brothers came and bowed down before him and his dream was fulfilled. Things had to be set in place and in order. But more importantly, God had some work to do in the hearts of Joseph and his brothers before He could fulfill the dream.

David's Cave time seemed SLOW. He was running and hiding from King Saul. It was nearly 15 years between the time that he had been anointed king and when he actually became king. This spiritual father that David tried to serve with great honor, persisted on trying to kill him. He was jealous and feared David would take over his throne. He knew in his heart that David was marked by God to be the next King, but He wasn't willing to train David up to take his place (or his son's place). A mature leader and true Father will train up Sons (and daughters) to take his place and desire for them to surpass him. This is a mark of true leadership. There is no competition and jealousy in the Kingdom of God.

David was also tested, so that God could transform him from an insecure, rejected shepherd boy into a king. God put a "Saul" in David's life to make sure that David wouldn't become a "Saul." God worked on David's heart for 15 years until He was certain David would not treat others the way that he had been treated. This testing pattern is found all throughout the Bible, and I believe God still does it today. (Ask me how I know)

Preparation seasons aren't pretty or fun, but they are necessary. Even Esther had to go through a year of preparation before she could even appear before the king.

We speak of the "suddenlies" of God, as if they happen rather instantaneously. The reality is, the finality may be quick, but the preparation is normally long and SLOW.

Abraham was told he would have a son. But It took 25 years for Issac to actually be birthed. There were things that God had to prepare Abraham for. His heart needed testing and proving. There were things that needed addressing and healing and other things that had to be set in motion. The timing of God isn't always our timing but it's perfect and right and always on time.

The easiest way to get through the process is to submit to the leading and direction of the Lord, have your heart in the right position, stay humble before the Lord and Don't fight it or try to avoid it. There are no shortcuts through the wilderness. It takes however long it takes to prepare you. Only God knows how long it will be. You can't shorten it, but you can lengthen it.

1Pe 5:6 (ESV) Humble yourselves, therefore, under the mighty hand of God so that at the proper time he may exalt you,

Surrender yourself under the mighty hand of God and allow Him to do what He does best: transform lives and change you into the person that He created you to be all along! You will be glad that you did!

Day 3
Arise My Warrior Bride

It is time we prepare for a war and a wedding at the same time.

Psalms 144:1 (ESV) Blessed be the Lord, my rock, who trains my hands for war, and my fingers for battle;"

There's an army arising, a remnant, a new breed of warriors, those who have been forged and reforged in the Fire of God and have been saturated in the Love of God.
They are resolute against the enemy, yet tender against the broken. Sometimes they must love them into the arms of the Father and sometimes they must snatch them out of hell's fire and the very hands of Satan himself. Holy Spirit always knows which way works best and they hear and obey the voice of God.

They have been plunged into the fiery furnace of affliction time and time again. Each time another layer is burned away and the refining process purifies and strengthens them as it continues to go deeper and deeper; burning away the dross and bringing forth a vessel refined for the Master's use. As they lay before the throne of God and present their bodies as living sacrifices unto the Lord, they are resolute in their love for the Father and determined to complete their kingdom assignments.

They are radical, intimate worshippers and lovers of Jesus. They crave the presence of God more than anything else. Consumed by

His love, they are presence driven and cry out for more of Him day and night. They are carriers of His glory and bearers of His presence. Revival and awakening burns within their bones as they release His Love and His Fire. They are the guardians of His sacred fire.

They are Kingdom Carriers. They know and understand the climate of their region and are determined to see it shift from darkness to light. They are called to conquer, occupy and possess the land, as they push back the darkness with His light.

They are totally sold out to God and called to release the Love of The Father, the Compassion of Christ and the Power of the Holy Spirit to the lost and dying world.

Their hearts have been placed in the very hands of God, to be healed, made whole and molded into the replicated Heart of God. They are determined to love what their Father loves and hate what He hates. They are called as agents of Love for the Kingdom of God and healers of the heart to release life and hope to the brokenhearted and freedom to the captives.

They will transform cities and shift regions by releasing the sound of their praise and worship and their powerful intercessory prayers and strong prophetic decrees into the atmosphere. Every sound that proceeds out of their mouth will seed the atmosphere with His Glory. It's all about **His Glory!**

They are the ones who will rise up when the Lord of Hosts is defiled and mocked and they will take down the giants in the land and in the hearts of the people.

This is the Warrior Bride. The warrior has been through the battle and warriors heal on the go. They pull the arrow out and keep going, determined to complete their assignment. Eager to hear, "Well done, My Child."

These are the true ones who have made a blood covenant with the Father and It's a lifelong commitment. The ring has been placed on their finger and the Key of David is in their hand. They have given Him their eternal "yes" and they will not turn back. The true Warrior Bride is Rising!

Take your place Mighty Warrior! It's time for the Army of God to arise and be who God created you to be! Your family, your region and your Nation is counting on you to step into your destiny!

Day 4
Time to Come Out of the Cave

Psa 143:5 (TPT) So I cried out to you, Lord, my only hiding place. You're all I have, my only hope in this life, my last chance for help. 6 Please listen to my heart's cry, for I am low and in desperate need of you! Rescue me from all those who persecute me, for I am no match for them. ***7 Bring me out of this dungeon so I can declare your praise!***

King David's cave was dark and cold and lonely. Yet there was a peace there: a safety in his solitude. Most days, his cave time drew him closer to his God, as he hid from the mad king who had tried to pin him to the wall as he served him. David was known to sing lullabies of deliverance to this mad king and others. Some of David's greatest trials occurred while in his cave. As David was hiding and distressed, he cried out to The Lord and as he did, Psalms were echoing around the cold damp walls; ricocheting like a boomerang stuck in a whirlwind. Those words changed his life and are still changing lives today. It was a place where David's heart was poured out in worship and God became his closest friend.

Sometimes when God is trying to mature you and birth something in you, He will stir you up, plant that seed and then take you to a dry and barren place and drop you off for a time of solitude to allow that seed to germinate. God once told me, "I called you alone and I saved you alone and now you have to learn to be alone with Me."

I'm sure David spent many days in tears as he questioned his so-called "anointing" by the great Prophet Samuel. I can just hear him, "This is not the life of a king. What was that anointing all about God? What about that oil the prophet poured on my head and those words he spoke over me in front of my brothers? Was that a cruel joke the prophet played on me? Have you really called me to be King of Israel? Have you forgotten me Lord? If I am really to be king, How long must I run and hide and fear the wrath of this mad king who seeks to destroy me?"

The anointing or calling on his life, set in motion a process that would take years to develop into what God designed it to be. Sometimes we have an encounter with God or get touched by Him and we expect things to instantly improve, and they do to some extent. At salvation, we set into motion the journey to our destiny. However, the struggles, trials and sufferings cannot be eliminated. There are some things that you can only learn from God through the fires, the trials and the sufferings.

As God, in all His sovereignty, is not bound by time or space. He will pick you up from where you are, show you the destination or the end result of what He's called you to be or do, then He will take you back to the beginning to start the process of developing you into what He has called you to be.

This process can take years. Issues of the heart must be dealt with. He also works on developing our character, our skills and our confidence. He usually has to convince us that it's really what He wants from us. Doubt and unbelief have to go. It can be challenging as God never calls you to do something that you have already mastered on your own.

Some call it the wilderness, or the threshing floor, but either way it's part of the process. Moses had his wilderness. Joseph had his dungeon. Daniel had his den. David had his cave. We all have our secret place where God takes us to in order to develop something in us that needs some incubation time that requires God to jealously brood over us in order to birth what He has placed inside us.

David's cave became The School of the Mighty Men. It was a place of deep communion with God and where broken men were made whole. It was a place of maturing and developing them into who the God of all creation had already destined them to be.

Everybody needs some cave time. We may prefer the sunshine, but from time to time we get the cave instead. The cave represents a place of dying to self, a place of testing, isolation and separation. In the cave, it's only you and God. You become totally dependent on The Lord for all your needs. It's a place of humbling and maturing.

Actually, God does some of His best work in caves; It can be a great place to get alone with God and birth new songs or poems or psalms or receive healing and wholeness over your life. There's an old saying that says, "Kings are made in Caves." I prefer to think of it more as a "birthing place" or a womb or cocoon. You might go in weak, wounded or broken; but God will bring you out healed, humbled and ready for battle. **You might go in as a misfit, but you will come out as a mighty man, if you stay the course.**

1Sa 22:1 David departed from there and escaped to the cave of Adullam. And when his brothers and all his father's house heard it, they went down there to him. 2 And everyone who was in distress, and everyone who was in debt, and everyone who was bitter in soul, gathered to him. And he became commander over them. And there were with him about four hundred men.

Welcome your cave time, don't complain and beg God to get you out of it. Ask God why you are there and what it is that He wants you to receive from it. Seek His face and worship Him through the entire process and you will become the mighty man or woman of God that He has created you to be.

1Ch 12:22 For from day to day men came to David to help him, until there was a great army, like an army of God.

It's time for God's Army to come out of the cave! Arise Warrior Bride!

Day 5
Child of God, There is Hope

Psa 147:3 (AMP) He heals the brokenhearted and binds up their wounds, curing their pains and their sorrows.

When all seems lost, when all seems hopeless, when you feel like you can't go on another day, there is hope. God is in the restoration business.

Most of us have been there at one time or another. We go through things that wound us and hurt us and break us down. Life is hard. There are trials and struggles. We stand at a place of decision, gripped by fear, knowing that the choice we make will affect our future, our children and our family forever. Yet, we struggle, still not knowing what to do or which way to turn. Without God's direction and guidance we are hopeless.

I am here to tell you, there is a better way. God can take your mess and turn it into a message. He can take everything you've been through in life and use it for His glory and His Kingdom. If you are willing to give it all to Him, He will restore you and transform you into the man or woman of God that He intended you to be all along. Yes, it takes humility. Yes, it takes trust. Yes, it takes faith. But when you do, He will pick up all the broken pieces and put them back together again. He will replace your hopelessness and despair with peace, love and joy.

Jesus came to heal the broken hearted and set the captives free. (Luke 4:18) He came to give us abundant life. But Satan, our enemy, came to steal, kill and destroy (John 10:10) and he will do just that if you allow him. He would like nothing more than to see you broken, addicted to drugs, alcohol or pornography and neglecting your kids and your finances in shambles. His desire is to keep you in a state of hopelessness and ready to end your own life. But God and all of Heaven says "NO"! You have eternity written in your book and God is on your side and here to help you fulfill your destiny.

We are in a war here and you must choose who's side we are on. It's either God's or Satan's. There is no other choice. You cannot remain neutral in a time of war. Fence straddlers are counted on the enemy's side in a time of war.

If you are tired of living a life of despair and misery, it's time to make a change. God has a plan for your life. He created you with purpose. He will restore you and give you hope and a future. He wants to see you walking in happiness and fulfilling everything that He has for you.

God created you with destiny in mind. Before you were born He marked you as His very own. There are Kingdom assignments that He has set aside specifically for you to do. He has a divine purpose for you being here. You are not an accident.

Jer. 1:5 (NLT) I knew you before I formed you in your mother's womb. Before you were born I set you apart and appointed you as my prophet to the nations.

So, Child of God, rise up! Surrender all your cares and troubles to God. Surrender your life to Him. He will never leave you or abandon you. He will fill you with His love and restore you. He will take away all of your sorrows and give you hope and happiness again.

John 15:16 (NLT) You didn't choose me. I chose you. I appointed you to go and produce lasting fruit, so that the Father will give you whatever you ask for, using my name."

He stands at the door of your heart and knocks, waiting for you to open up and let Him in. (Rev3:20) Why don't you let Him in today. I promise you, it will be the best decision you have ever made. Your life will never be the same. No matter what you have done or where you have been or what you have been through, Jesus is always there waiting with open arms, ready to receive you. Come to Him now and watch what He will do with you and through YOU!

Day 6
The Characteristics of God's True Army

Isa 42:13 (NASB) The LORD will go forth like a warrior, He will arouse His zeal like a man of war. He will utter a shout, yes, He will raise a war cry. He will prevail against His enemies.

The Lord God himself is a warrior. He is the first of the mighty men and calls us to be like Him; Strong and full of zeal and passion for the things of God.

God has been wandering to and fro throughout the earth looking for a people through whom He can make Himself strong and show Himself mighty. He's looking for Kings and Priests, warriors and champions; Those who are not afraid or intimidated by the enemy but trust God and believe what the Word of God says.

Let me share with you some of the characteristics of God's true army that He is raising up for this hour.

- *1.* **Totally Surrendered to God-** We are to become a walking, talking, living sacrifice.

Rom 12:1 (ESV) I appeal to you therefore, brothers, by the mercies of God, to present your bodies as a living sacrifice, holy and acceptable to God, which is your spiritual worship.

- **2. Obedient-** God calls for total obedience. To obey is better than sacrifice. Obedience Is the opposite of rebellion, which leads to witchcraft. (1 Sam 15:22-23)

- **3. Unoffendable-** We must always respond in a spirit of Love and under the direction and guidance of the Lord. Our actions should always be based on the Word of God, not on what other people say or what they do or our emotions.

- **4. Courageous** - We are commanded to be courageous, it's not a suggestion. We are to walk in a spirit of boldness, yet with a spirit of humility, totally under full surrender to God's Holy Spirit.

Jos 1:9 (ESV) Have I not commanded you? Be strong and courageous. Do not be frightened, and do not be dismayed, for the LORD your God is with you wherever you go."

- **5. Trust In God-** *Job 13:15 (KJV) Though He slay me, I will trust Him.*

- **6. Healed-** We must be healed and made whole and have nothing in common with the enemy.

John 14:30 (AMP) I will not talk with you much more, for the prince (evil genius, ruler) of the world is coming. And he has no claim on Me. [He has nothing in common with Me; there is nothing in Me that belongs to him, and he has no power over Me.]

- **7. Perseverance-** Never give up. Never quit. The enemy's strategy is to force you to back up. He works through fear and intimidation. He's a bully. Don't give up on your promises. There is victory in the perseverance. Sometimes you just have to outlast your enemies.

- **8. My Praise is a Weapon-** We must be trained in spiritual warfare, yet our focus is not on the enemy, but on God and His goodness.

Psalm 61:8 (TPT) My praises will fill the heavens forever, fulfilling my vow to make everyday a love gift to you.

- **9. Having a Strong Spirit of Discernment-** This is absolutely necessary or we will be deceived.

- **10. Walk in Honor-** Honoring others above ourselves and honoring God releases His Glory. As a matter of fact, Honor is the highest form of spiritual warfare. It is a weapon that Satan hates. Unfortunately, it's become a lost art that desperately needs to be restored.

- **11. Passionate, laid down lovers-** Love sick warriors. Addicted to His presence. We must be determined to steward His presence with purity, integrity and sensitivity to Holy Spirit: Glory Carriers who will challenge others to come up higher.

Deu 6:5 (ESV) You shall love the LORD your God with all your heart and with all your soul and with all your might.

- **12. Identity-** We must Know who we are in Christ.

*Rom 8:14 (ESV) For all who are led by the **Spirit of God are sons of God.** 15 For you did not receive the **spirit of slavery** to fall back into fear, but you have received the Spirit of **adoption as sons**, by whom we cry, "Abba! Father!"*

David stood up to Goliath and took him on, confidently knowing that the uncircumcised Philistine would fall. David knew he would defeat him because he had a promise from God that said he would be king. David ran toward the giant, not away from him; he stood firm on the promises of God. The Lord had said he would be king one day and he wasn't king yet, so he couldn't die yet. He was confident in what God had called him to do and knew that God would prevail.

Once we really understand our purpose and our identity, our lives will radically change. God is looking for those who will surrender it all to Him. He is raising up an army of warriors who are fully submitted and surrendered to accomplishing His agenda on earth. Will you give God your "yes" and surrender your life to Him? Will you enlist in His Army?

Day 7
Overcoming Fear and Walking in Power and Authority

2Ti 1:7 (KJV) For God hath not given us the spirit of fear, but of power and of love and of a sound mind.

Fear is real. It can consume your every thought and overtake you if you allow it. Fear comes from Satan and is the opposite of Faith. The Word of God teaches us that faith will overcome fear. When you feel fear rising up inside of you, recognize it for what it is and then do not receive it, cast it down, knowing that it comes from Satan, not from God.

The only way the enemy can defeat you is through deceiving your mind. You must learn to stand on God's Word and take authority over these things that come to destroy you. When you learn to do this, you will have peace and His promises will come to pass in your lives.

Hosea 4:6 says, (ESV) My people are destroyed for lack of knowledge...

What you don't know CAN hurt you. When you learn to war with The Word, you will have a very valuable tool needed to overcome the enemy. The Word is powerful and sharper than any two edged sword. A two edged sword cuts in both directions; going in and coming out.

Your foundation must be based on a relationship with Jesus Christ, not religion or tradition or someone else's beliefs. If that is your foundation, it is faulty and it will crumble when trials and tribulations come your way.

Satan plots against the children of God. Just like a lion in the wild, he hides and he waits for the opportune time when his prey is distracted or becomes isolated, weak, or disconnected from the flock and the shepherd and then he attacks.

1Pe 5:8 (ESV) Be sober-minded; be watchful. Your adversary the devil prowls around like a roaring lion, seeking someone to devour.

Satan has no creative power. He can only twist or counterfeit what God has already created. He comes to pervert and distort the TRUTH of God. Satan is a bully and he operates on FEAR and intimidation and manipulation. God's kingdom operates on Love, Faith and truth. God builds you up while Satan's tactic is to tear you down. They are total opposites.

As children of God, we can be completely free from fear. We don't have to fall into Satan's trap. We are children of the Most High God. When we have the Holy Spirit living in us, we have the same power in us that raised Jesus from the dead! (Rom8:11) Let that sink in!

Once you begin to understand the authority that you have in Christ, as a believer and a Son or daughter of the Most High God, you can become completely free from fear. When you do... watch out... You will start to see major victories in your life!

If you have accepted Jesus Christ as your Lord and Savior, then you are a Son (or daughter) of The Living God. You are also an heir to the kingdom of God. An heir is someone who receives property or an inheritance, or a rank, title or office because of their ancestry lineage or they may be entitled to reign or take over a certain role or position because of their bloodline. That is YOU, Child of God. You are not an orphan.

*Galatians 4:4-7 (NLT) 4 But when the right time came, God sent his Son, born of a woman, subject to the law. 5 God sent him to buy freedom for us who were slaves to the law, so that he could adopt us **as his very own children.** 6 And because we are his children, God has sent the Spirit of his Son into our hearts, prompting us to call out, "Abba, Father." 7 Now you are no longer a slave but God's own child. And since you are his child, **God has made you his heir.***

If you were the son of a king in the natural, what would your life be like? Would you worry about clothes to wear or food to eat or money to spend? No, you would have more than your needs met; You would ask for something and it would be given to you. You would speak and laws would be made or carried out. When you grasp this concept, that YOU are a **Son of the Living God,** your life will radically change.

Rom 8:14 (ESV) For all who are led by the Spirit of God are sons of God.

For me personally, I lived with fear for many years. But once I truly discovered who I really was in Christ and understood my God given identity, my life radically changed. I no longer walked in fear. I walked in faith; knowing that God was in control and that He loved me and would provide for me.

Sometimes we have to be taught how to stand and how to walk in Christ. We can't always rely on others (or even the Church) to meet our needs. We have to be equipped with the knowledge and the tools we need to overcome. Pray and ask God to help you and to lead you. You can do this! I believe in you! God has already given you the ability to overcome. The overcomer lives on the inside of you. Victory is your destiny.

I suggest that you begin a quest to discover your true identity and decide right now that you will not stop until you find it. Ask God who He created you to be and allow Him to mold you and shape you into the person that He created you to be all along. Give Him your heart: Place it in His hands. Close your eyes right now and see yourself doing this. Tell God that your heart belongs to Him and then give it to Him. Go ahead, I'm waiting. And He's waiting too.

Now, go on a quest to search out the scriptures and discover who God says you are, not who the world says you are or not even who you say that you are. Don't settle for anything less than who God says you are. Allow that Rhema word to come alive and speak to you. Your destiny is waiting for you to manifest into the fullness of who God created you to be. All creation is waiting on you to manifest as the mighty warrior that you are. So, I say, "Mighty Warrior, Arise and Come Forth!"

I love the way The Passion Translation says it.

Romans 8:19 (TPT) The entire universe is standing on tiptoe, yearning to see the unveiling of God's glorious sons and daughters!

Wow! How does that make you feel? To think the entire universe is waiting on YOU! Tell all fear to go, in Jesus name and let faith arise! You are destined to live a life of victory! The cloud of witnesses are cheering right now. I see them peering over Heaven's edge, saying "You can do this!"

Joshua 1:9 (NLT) This is my command—be strong and courageous! Do not be afraid or discouraged. For the Lord your God is with you wherever you go.

Child of God, rise up! You are not alone.

Day 8
Offense Will Teach or Kill, You Choose

Offense is a matter of the heart. Offense will kill you. It will cripple you. It's a trap. It's the bait of Satan. The enemy sends it to stop you from moving forward into your assignment. There are great deceptive powers in offense.

Wherever there's a religious spirit you'll find offense. If you find yourself getting offended easily, ask God to kill that religious spirit in you! It is impossible to walk in love if you are offended and Faith won't work if you don't have love.

Matt 24: 10 (KJV) And then shall many be offended, and shall betray one another, and shall hate one another.

People who are offended, don't usually even know they are offended. They are so focused on the wrong that was done to them, they are blind to it and in denial. They play the victim and become angry and bitter if it's not dealt with.

Pro 18:19 (AMP) A brother offended is harder to be won over than a strong city, and [their] contentions separate them like the bars of a castle.

When people walk in Offense, you will find them also carrying anger, jealousy, resentment, strife, bitterness and hatred. It will continue to get worse over time until they find themselves totally consumed with their hurt and pain. Bitter people aren't pleasant to be around. Pride will take over and keep them from admitting their true condition. It will always be someone else's fault, in their eyes.

Jesus said, Offense will come!! It is not a question of IF, but WHEN?

Luke 17:1 (KJV) "It is impossible but that offenses will come; But woe unto him through whom they come!"

Offense comes when someone doesn't react or respond to you the way that you think they should have. You fabricate *false* expectations of them and then get angry, upset or insulted when they don't live up to it. Don't be like the elder brother.

Luk 15:28 (ISV) Then the older son became angry and wouldn't go into the house. So his father came out and began to plead with him.

Offense and jealousy breed anger and resentment and cause you to point out all their faults and focus on their sins. You will want to harm or curse or even kill the other person. It will cause you to be blinded to God's truth and lose your relationship with God and the very one He has connected you with. You will become bitter and full of anger and hate.

Mat 24:10 (AMP) And then many will be offended and repelled (to push back or back away from) *and will begin to distrust and desert [Him Whom they ought to trust and obey] and will stumble and*

fall away and betray one another and pursue one another with
hatred.

You will try and destroy the very one that God sent to you to
mature you or help you.
Don't fall into Satan's trap. Look what happened to some of
Jesus's disciples.

John 6:66 (AMP) After this, many of His disciples drew back
(returned to their old associations) and no longer accompanied
Him.

When you harbor offense against your leader, you will draw back
and return to your old ways and abort your God given destiny.
Offense will cause you to abort your calling and to walk away
from your promises of God. Offense will cut off the flow of the
Holy Spirit moving in your life for you and those around you.
Offense will lead you to death and destruction.

John the Baptist had the ultimate test over offense. (Matt 11)
John was in prison. He had spent his whole life devoted to
preparing the way for Jesus. He could have at this point said,
"Bump this.... don't you know what I did for you? I spent years
telling people about you, crying out as a lone voice, wearing camel
hair and eating honey and wild locusts, I could have steak and
taters.... and now Here I am in prison and now you are out there
doing all the cool stuff. That's not fair..."

When you compare yourself to others and don't walk in your gift,
but covet other people's gifts, then you become offended. But

Jesus said, "go tell John don't be offended at me. I'm doing what you prophesied I would do."

Being offended will affect your spiritual eyesight, it will hinder you from seeing the truth, it will cause you to believe a lie. It will block you from receiving what God has for you.

When you take on offense, you are walking in the flesh. You will fail to believe and trust and have faith. You will take on doubt, insecurities and fear. It will cause you to draw back from God or your leader or whoever you have offense against. You will walk away from your calling if you harbor offense in your heart.

Offense is a great teacher though. Learn to use it to your advantage. It will Bring an awareness to the areas of your heart and your life that you have not yet surrendered to God. When you feel it rising up, you must humble yourself, repent and ask God to forgive you for harboring offense toward that person.

When someone says something or does something you don't like or agree with and you feel that offense rising up within you, that anger, that resentment and that need to defend or attack, or give them a piece of your mind, then you have taken on that offense.

Offense will give way to the spirit of rebellion. It will teach you the areas of your heart and spiritual development that need to be healed or corrected. Rebellious people are offended people who never got healed. There is a spirit of offense all across the earth right now. Satan loves to use this to keep people in bondage.

How do we overcome? Always take the low road, never think of yourself more highly than others, always look at yourself as a servant. Don't take things personal. Recognize it for what it is and don't let the enemy use it to destroy you. Realize it can be a tool that God can use to bring you to the place where He wants you to be. When you feel offense rising up, go to God and go to that person. Don't harbor it. Do whatever is necessary to overcome it.

Don't allow it to wound you, allow it to heal you. Let every assault come to work on you and in you. It's all about perspective. Offense is a teacher. It will show you how mature or immature you really are. It will show you the position of your heart.

Will you pray or will you attack? Will you bless those who curse you or will you tear down and gossip? Will you change your perspective and use offense as a tool to mature you, or will it be a dagger to destroy you? It's your choice.

Day 9
Praise Your Way Through The Sufferings

Psalm 30:5b (NLT) Weeping may last through the night, but joy comes with the morning.

When we become a Christian, we should expect to have tests and trials. It's all part of your walk and God's plan. God never said it would be easy. Jesus' walk wasn't easy; neither were the disciples or Paul's or anyone else's who did great things for God. However, God has given us tools and strategies to help us through times of trials and sufferings.

1Pe 4:12 (ESV) Beloved, do not be surprised at the fiery trial when it comes upon you to test you, as though something strange were happening to you. 13 But rejoice insofar as you share Christ's sufferings, that you may also rejoice and be glad when his glory is revealed.

We have to learn to rejoice in the midst of the storms; Praise God and worship Him through the storms and speak life over ourselves and our circumstances. Our Praise and worship and dance are all weapons against the enemy and our voice is a mighty weapon too. The Word of God is sharper than any two-edged sword. We can speak life or death, blessings or cursings. If we only knew the true power of our words, we could move mountains, calm storms and change lives.

While the world says go ahead and be a lover of pleasure, do your own thing, if you like it and it feels good, just do it. The Word says, deny yourself, pick up your cross and follow me. This indicates that there will be a shedding; a leaving behind; a shaking loose of some things and people in order for you to truly walk with God.

It's in those trying times that you are drawn closer to God and strengthened to become the person that He intended you to be. It's during those times that your character is perfected into the image of Christ. Every step is a necessary preparation process to make you durable and pliable, a vessel of honor, to be used by God for His service.

Suffering for Christ is not a bad thing. It may not be pleasurable at the moment, but afterwards the reward is great. As you look back, you will see God had a purpose for your pain and He will use everything for His glory if you allow Him. Nothing will be wasted or lost.

*James 1:2 (TPT) My fellow believers, when it seems as though you are facing nothing but difficulties, see it as an **invaluable opportunity** to experience the greatest joy that you can! 3 For you know that when your faith is tested it stirs up power within you to endure all things. 4 And then as your endurance grows even stronger it will release perfection into every part of your being until there is nothing missing and nothing lacking.*

I love that verse! If you will allow Him, God will take and build a ministry out of your misery and mistakes. God does not use our past to disqualify us from our future. Forgive yourself and let God mold you into what he wants you to be. He isn't disappointed or mad at you; He loves you and cares deeply for you. He came to give you hope and a future!

Jer 29:11-13 (NLT) For I know the plans I have for you," says the Lord. "They are plans for good and not for disaster, to give you a future and a hope. In those days when you pray, I will listen. If you look for me wholeheartedly, you will find me."

Today is your day to shift and change. The suffering you have endured wasn't meant to destroy you, it was meant to empower you. Your praise is a mighty weapon in the arsenal of God. Get your praise on and watch your enemies be scattered!

Psalms 68:1 (AMP) Let God arise, and His enemies be scattered....

Don't focus on the storm. Focus on God and His goodness. Satan will try and beat you down. That's his nature. Don't give him the time of day. He started off in the garden as a serpent, but by the time he gets to Revelation, he's a dragon. Somebody's been feeding him. Don't you dare! Put all your focus on God and let Him fight your battles for you!

Deu 3:22 (AMP) You shall not fear them, for the Lord your God shall fight for you.

Day 10
The Power of the Word

Psa 12:6 (AMP) The words and promises of the Lord are pure words, like silver refined in an earthen furnace, purified seven times over.

The word came from heaven declaring that Jesus was the Son of God and Immediately the devourer came to steal the Word. Satan always comes to steal the seed. He wants to steal and devour you and your inheritance.

Mar 4:4 (ESV) And as he sowed, some seed fell along the path, and the birds came and devoured it.

The Son of God was tempted by Satan to operate outside of the Word of God, But He did not. His flesh didn't react to His situation. He didn't forget who He was and why He was there. It's not always what we see or how we feel that we should respond or react to. Jesus didn't get caught up in His circumstances; He stood on the written Word of God. He declared and decreed the Word of the Lord into His situation.

"It is Written" echoed throughout all the wilderness as Jesus declared "Man shall not live by bread alone." We must not only declare and decree, We must mix our faith with The Word. Notice how Satan didn't give up easily. He came again and he tried to place doubt. "IF" you are really the son of God. Satan is still, to this day, trying to place doubt in the Sons of God by stealing their identity and authority.

Thank God, Jesus didn't buy into it. He was not deceived. He was not moved out of the assignment of God. He used the Word as His weapon to fight His battle. Even though Satan didn't just give up quickly, after 3 attacks he left for a season. (Luke 4::13)

Heaven rejoiced that day as Jesus overcame Satan. There was great victory for the Kingdom of God and a death blow for the kingdom of darkness. I think that Jesus took back those things lost in the garden as He overcame the lust of the eyes, the lust of the flesh and the pride of life. Jesus stepped into His ministry in power and authority, ready to complete His earthly assignment.

Luk 4:14 (AMP) Then Jesus went back full of and under the power of the [Holy] Spirit into Galilee, and the fame of Him spread through the whole region round about.

The same is true with us. Don't expect Satan to stop harassing you after the first battle. God uses warfare to strengthen you and give you the ability to endure hardships and to persevere. God needs to know that you will stand even when all hell comes against you. He needs to know what it will take for you to quit. In other words, How solid are you in your commitment to Him. He will test you to reveal the true position of your heart.

The victory comes when your faith in God's Word is greater than your faith in your situation. Satan's plan, as it has been since the beginning, Is to discredit and disprove the Word of God. But we must be like Jesus and determine that we will not be moved. We just need to get to that place where we say, "If God said it, then it is truth and I will plant my feet on that Rock and stand firm. I will not be swayed by the voice of the enemy or his false promises of fame, fortune or power."

Why does the enemy fight the Word of God so hard? Because he knows that once you step out into the realm of faith in God's Word, that he is a defeated foe. When you truly start fully believing and obeying the Word, then God's power will be released in your life for His Glory and then there is NO stopping you! Satan knows the power of The Word and he knows that Jesus gave you all of His authority when He returned to the Father.

Remember that Jesus had just come out of His wilderness experience where the Word of the Lord was being tested as to whether or not He was truly the Son of God. Once this test was over, He began His ministry in the power of the Holy Spirit. Satan never tempted Jesus in this area again. The victory had been won. Once Jesus received the victory, He remained victorious. Jesus came as our example. He was anointed with the Holy Spirit and then he was tested. (Sound familiar?) He allowed us to see that everyone goes through a period where the Word of God is tested in their lives.

We serve an infinite God who has no beginning and He has no end. He will give you as much of Himself as you will allow Him. Determine in your heart that you will not stop seeking and searching after more of Him. Your life will never be the same once you encounter The True and Living God.

Matthew 5:6 (ESV) Blessed are those who hunger and thirst for righteousness, for they shall be satisfied.

The only way to walk in a victorious Christian lifestyle is to stay in the power and authority of God's Word through Jesus Christ. Don't be moved by your circumstances, or by what you see or feel. Learn to stand on the Word of God and see the salvation of the Lord.

Find those promises in the scriptures and stand on them as if they are true gold; for they are. For example, When you are battling the enemy over your children, Stand on this:

Isa 44:3 (ESV) For I will pour water on the thirsty land, and streams on the dry ground; I will pour my Spirit upon your offspring, and my blessing on your descendants.

Start believing what God's Word says about you and your situation. Stop believing the lies that Satan has fed man from the beginning of time. The reason Satan attacks the Word is that he knows if you war with the Word, you will win. Find a promise in God's Word and stand on it. Determine for yourself that if God said it, then you are going to believe it, regardless of what you see or how you feel. It's not what you see, but what God says.

Job 22:28 (KJV) Thou shalt also decree a thing, and it shall be established unto thee: and the light shall shine upon thy ways.

Rom 4:17 (ESV) As it is written, "I have made you the father of many nations"—in the presence of the God in whom he believed, **who gives life to the dead and calls into existence the things that do not exist.**

When you start to put your faith in Jesus Christ and His Word, your life will radically shift and change. The supernatural power of God will break through those hard places in your life and give you the strength and power that you need to overcome. Don't take my word for it, take HIS Word for it! Put it to the test today.

Day 11
Go To Your Room!

Do you have a war room? (Also known as a prayer closet or the secret place) If not, you better make one. Prayer is the key that moves the hand of God. We are in a war and we need a strategic plan to come against and defeat the enemy. He is trying to destroy this country and our families. Satan wants to tear down the very structure that God put in place. Prepare yourselves people of God, for your destiny and the destiny of this nation, hangs in the balance right now.

God is raising up secret weapons formed and fashioned in the secret place. You, my friend, were born to be a stealth bomber to destroy the works of the enemy with the power of Almighty God. You are a mighty weapon for the Kingdom of God.

You are in a battle. Your destiny, and your family's destiny depends on your ability to fight the good fight of faith. The Word says that there is life and death in the power of the tongue. We have to learn to war with the Word of God and our words or we will be overcome by the enemy.

Someone dear to me once told me, "What you have in your life is what you have spoken and nothing is created in the spirit realm without words." We have to learn to speak it out, and when we do, then we can see the hand of God move and release life and freedom.

We must learn to speak the words of life and liberty and come against the enemy who comes to steal, kill and destroy. He's not playing games. He's out to destroy you, your family, your health, your finances and anything else he can get his hands on.

But we have been given authority over him. *Luke 10:19 (ESV) says, "Behold, I have given you authority to tread on serpents and scorpions, and over all the power of the enemy, and nothing shall hurt you."*

Jesus didn't leave us empty handed. He gave us everything that we will ever need to defeat the enemy and overcome every problem or situation that we encounter in life.

In Eph 6 He explains The Armor of God. We must put it on and wear it continuously, so the enemy cannot overtake us. He may sling his fiery darts, spew his foul words, but they will not penetrate our armor when we are girded up.

Immediately after explaining the armor, He tells us to go and speak it out boldly.

*Eph 6:19 (ESV) and also for me, that words may be given to me in **opening my mouth boldly** to proclaim the mystery of the gospel, 20 for which I am an ambassador in chains, that I may **declare it boldly**, as I ought to speak.*

Satan comes to deceive and he will deceive even the very elect, if we are not prepared for his attacks and learn to come against them properly. The word of God is powerful. It is a mighty weapon in the arsenal of God.

Heb 4:12 (ESV) For the word of God is living and active, sharper than any two-edged sword, piercing to the division of soul and of spirit, of joints and of marrow, and discerning the thoughts and intentions of the heart.

Jesus defeated Satan in the wilderness by speaking The Word. That was an example that He gave us and He expects us to do the same.

I'm sure if we all sat down and talked openly, we could all remember some hurtful words spoken over us as a child; words that some well meaning person spoke to you that pierced your heart. Perhaps You still remember how your Daddy said, " If you would lose some weight you'd be pretty." Or maybe a teacher said, " you are just not as smart as your brother."

For some of you, those words still haunt you today. Well, if the negative words can do that much damage, just think about how much good the positive ones can do.

Jesus came to set the captives free, to release life and freedom to the people, to destroy the works of the enemy and to teach us to do the same. Don't live another day holding grudges against those who hurt you. Life is too short and the Kingdom of God needs you healed and set free and advancing the Kingdom. Forgive that person today, let it go and begin to live a life of freedom and happiness and joy in the Lord.

Stand up and speak out words of life that will destroy the works of the enemy and bring life to you and the people around you that you love and that need love. Jesus died for you so that you could have abundant life.

Psalms 40:1-3 (NLT) I waited patiently for the Lord to help me, and he turned to me and heard my cry. He lifted me out of the pit of despair, out of the mud and the mire. He set my feet on solid ground and steadied me as I walked along. He has given me a new song to sing, a hymn of praise to our God. Many will see what he has done and be amazed. They will put their trust in the Lord.

Jesus is our rock and our fortress. He's our savior, deliverer, healer, provider and much more. Allow Him to work in your life, to mold you into the person that He intended you to be all along. He has a divine assignment prepared for you and it's perfect just for you. Don't miss out on your destiny that awaits you. God is calling His Bride -the church, to awake from her slumber and take her place in the Kingdom of God.

That's you Mighty one! Rise up and speak life and watch God conquer and move those things that have held you hostage for so long. Freedom is now within your reach! Grab it and hold on to it like the horns on the altar.

Day 12
The Transforming Power of God

2Co 5:17 (KJV) Therefore if any man be in Christ, he is a new creature: old things are passed away; behold, all things are become new.

When God comes into a person's life, things change. You cannot get in the presence of God and remain the same. He loves you too much to leave you where He finds you. He wants the very best for you. You are His beloved child. He will renew your mind and cause you to change your way of thinking. He will heal you of old hurts and wounds and give you purpose and true happiness that can only come from God.

Each one of us is born with a void in our hearts that only God can fill. We usually FEEL that void and then we try to FILL it with all the wrong things. Some go after drugs, alcohol, wrong relationships, pornography, become workaholics, gluttons, or numerous other destructive behaviors. They are desperately trying to FILL that void that can only be FILLED with the Love of God. But God is here today to FILL that void and take you on a journey that will radically transform your entire life and all those around you. The future of your children and your entire family depends upon where you go from here. You have the ability, through Christ, to change the destiny of your people; those in your circle of influence and those in your path on this journey called life.

Romans 6:6 (NLT) We know that our old sinful selves were crucified with Christ so that sin might lose its power in our lives. We are no longer slaves to sin.

God is a transforming God. He will bring hope to the hopeless. He will turn a drug addict into a preacher. He will take an alcoholic and transform them into a counselor. He will take a depressed young mother and turn her into a happy, loving and caring mother. He will take a suicidal person and restore peace and joy to them and give them a purpose and a reason to live.

All God needs is for you to say "yes" to Him. He so desires to see you fulfilling your destiny. He stands at the door of your heart and knocks. He's waiting right now for someone reading this to open the door of their heart and let Him in. I guarantee that when you do, your life will never be the same. Go ahead, ask Him in right now. I dare you.

He will give you victory over your struggles. He will restore the joy in your life. He will set you free from addictive behaviors. God is still in the miracle working business and right now, you are His miracle. He is working on transforming you into that mighty warrior that He has called you to be.

Jesus came to set the captives free and to heal the broken hearted. He came to redeem mankind and destroy the works of the devil and He is drawing you to Himself right now. Do you feel Him? Don't resist. Just pause right now and tell Him that you receive Him as Lord of your life and give Him permission to transform you into who you were created to be. That's what He does best. Don't wait another day. Choose this day whom you will serve. It will be the best decision that you ever made. Write it down. Mark this day on your calendar. Your life will never be the same.

Your life will begin to have purpose and God will begin the process of transforming you into the person that He intended you to be all along. It's not too late. Give Him your "Yes", your "eternal yes". Ask Him to come into your heart and renew your mind and to change you to be like Him. After all, He made you in His very own image. Life changes you but He will change you back.

We are called to be imitators of God. (Eph 5:1) He's coming back for His church, His Bride, without spot, wrinkle or blemish; (Eph 5:27) Those who have been purged in His refining fire and baked in His never ending Love, find themselves turned into a different person. As you allow Him to transform you into His image, you will begin to look and act and walk and talk like Him. A true Son becomes a reflection of his Father.

Say Yes Lord! Come into my heart. I want to be like you. Change me, renew me, make me into the person that you created me to be! Get ready! Your journey begins today! He's waiting on you and It's an amazing ride!

Day 13
Rise up Child of God .... You Are Not a Slave but a Son!

Do you know your Father? I'm not talking about your earthly Father, I'm talking about your Heavenly Father. When you accept Jesus as your Lord and Savior, you are adopted into the family of God. You are no longer an orphan or a slave; You are a Son of the Living God. (It's not gender based. If men can be part of the Bride then women can be Sons of God)

Gal 4:6 (ESV) And because you are sons, God has sent the Spirit of his Son into our hearts, crying, "Abba! Father!" 7 So you are no longer a slave, but a son, and if a son, then an heir through God.

An orphan mindset will cause you to live a life of uncertainty and apprehension; always struggling with your true identity and constantly not being able to trust or love. You will find yourself having a fear of being rejected and not having the ability to open up your heart to receive or give love.

Think about an orphan on the street. They have no home or place of security. They are driven by fear and are loyal to whoever meets their needs at the moment. They may feel as though they have no value or purpose.

But a true son knows where his home is. He is safe and secure there. He is not led by fear, but by faith. He is loyal to his father at all costs, because he knows his father will provide for him and protect him. A true son also knows that his father will reveal his purpose and leave an inheritance for him.

John 1:12 (NLT) But to all who believed him and accepted him, he gave the right to become children of God.

When we come into the family of God, we must learn to trust God and open up our hearts to Him. We can't let the storms, setbacks, and disappointments of life make us afraid to trust and afraid to receive God's love. When we do not love ourselves, we feel unlovable and find it difficult, if not impossible, to believe that anyone else could love us, including God.

Ephesians 1:5 (NLT) God decided in advance to adopt us into his own family by bringing us to himself through Jesus Christ. This is what he wanted to do, and it gave him great pleasure.

I once read a story about a baby bird that had fallen out of its nest. It wasn't just any bird, it was a baby eagle. A mother chicken found the little bird and took pity on the abandoned eaglet and raised it as her own.

As it grew, the young eagle pecked and shuffled along with the other chickens, having never realized that life could be any different; having never known that he was not a chicken, but he was an eagle.

One day he looked up into the sky and saw an eagle soaring high and he marveled. He was amazed at such a majestic bird, not knowing all along that within him, he possessed that same power and ability to soar, not because he deserved it, but because his Father was an eagle.

As Sons and Daughters of God, we are created in His image and we should bear the resemblance of our Father. But if we are like the baby eagle, we will live with an orphan mindset and NEVER fulfill our destiny. We will live a life full of our very own fabricated limitations that we create in our mind and with our own way of thinking.

When we have an orphan mindset, the thought of God loving us seems too good to be true and much more than we deserve. However, God doesn't love us because we deserve it. He loves us because that's who He is. God is love. God Himself said, in *Jeremiah 31:3 (NLT) "I have loved you, my people, with an everlasting love. With unfailing love I have drawn you to myself."*

When God welcomes you into His family and you receive Him as your Father, He takes away your orphan spirit and adopts you as His very own. You can come boldly to Him, realizing that He is your loving Father and He accepts you as His Child.

1Jn 3:1 (ESV) See what kind of love the Father has given to us, that we should be called children of God; and so we are.

The Father loves us. We cannot earn more of his love and we cannot lose his love. The most quoted verse says, "For God SO **loved** the world that He **gave** His only begotten son," (John 3:16 KJV) and God gave everything to Jesus who in return gave it to us.

Jesus said in John 16:15 (ESV) All that the Father has is mine; therefore I said that he will take what is mine and declare it to you.

So rise up mighty men and women of God and take your place in the Kingdom of God. You are an heir to the Almighty God who created the universe!

Rom 8:19 (ESV) For the creation waits with eager longing for the revealing (or manifestation) of the sons of God.

The Passion Translation puts it this way: *"The entire universe is standing on tiptoe, yearning to see the unveiling of God's glorious sons and daughters!"* That's YOU! *(Romans 8:19 TPT)*

Take your place Child of God! All creation is eagerly waiting and All of Heaven is eagerly waiting for you to step into your destiny.

Day 14
Competition Kills

Rivalry and Competition produce jealousy, envy, anger and rebellion. James 3:16 says (AMP) *"For wherever there is jealousy (envy) and contention (rivalry and selfish ambition), there will also be confusion (unrest, disharmony, rebellion) and all sorts of evil and vile practices."*

I have often wondered why there is so much jealousy and disharmony amongst the body of Christ. I thought we were all working for the Kingdom of God? In 1 Cor 12, Christ compares the church to a body. He says there are many members or parts, but one body and that's how it should be with the body of Christ. Each part has a proper place and has a very important function, yet by itself it cannot accomplish much. Each part is dependent upon every other part doing what they are designed to do.

When you operate out of a spirit of competition, you contaminate what God is trying to do. Look what it did to Cain and Abel. It led to murder.

Genesis 4 tells the story of how Cain rose up and killed his brother. Then he lied to God and became a vagabond and a wanderer. If harbored, this spirit will cause you to not be able to connect and align properly in the body. Your critical spirit will lead to pride and rebellion and you will become a renegade as you see yourself better than or above others. You will think that what you bring to the Lord is superior to others.

In our physical bodies, there is no competition between the feet and the hands. That would just be dumb wouldn't it? What if the foot says, "I want to be a hand." If you attached your foot to your hand would it function as well? How about I take my eye and put it where my foot goes? Or take my heart and place it where my liver is? No, it wouldn't work at all that way.

In the same way, there is no room for competition in the body of Christ. When you are truly walking with the Lord, you will not compete against other believers or churches. Competition breeds strife, which is one of the things God hates. Competition sows discord among the brethren. It will cause you to talk about others and criticize them and try and turn others against them. It will cause you to release cursings instead of blessings on people.

When each person is doing what God has called them to do, there will be no competition. You will honor each other and lift them up and value what they do.

Each person has a place and an assignment in the body of Christ. You have already been graced for that assignment by God. When you try and step out of your graced place, it becomes a sloppy mess. How would it work if you walked on your eye or you tried to eat with your ear? It wouldn't work that way at all because that's not how God designed it to be.

I know that sounds funny, but that's what it looks like when we are out of place and not functioning in the body of Christ like God created us to function. We each need to learn to be what God has created us to be and to function in the fullness of what He has for us.

Don't look around at others and compare yourself to them or you will become critical and start looking for anything in them that will make them look bad and you look good. Don't become critical and start trying to correct others by telling them what they are doing wrong or what they should do differently. That's not your place.

This works for us individually and also corporately and is for churches and denominations as well. We should all be focused on Jesus and allow The Holy Spirit to lead and guide us and not be critical of others because God gave them a different assignment than He gave you.

Gal 5:15 (AMP) But if you bite and devour one another [in partisan strife - partisan is to fight against one another in secret], be careful that you [and your whole fellowship] are not consumed by one another.

The spirit of competition strives to be number one. It tears down others with evil words. We've seen a lot of this in the church. It's a stench in the nostrils of God. He hates it. It causes character assassination, broken hearts and even wars. It will cause people to hate God and the Church.

God does not desire that you live this way. It's time to Uncover these sins in your heart and discover How to rightly respond to those who treat you this way.

Every believer has an assignment for the kingdom. God helps us all to stay where we are called. God has the perfect place for you. It's designed especially for you. Nobody else. It's God's desire for you to discover what makes you unique.

God is calling for unity or a oneness among His believers. I hate to disappoint you, but there will not be denominations in Heaven. So we might want to learn to get along now and honor each other for the gifts of God that we each have.

Everything that God has placed His seal on is important. What you carry for the Body of Christ is valuable. God has a specific assignment designed only for you. Continue to seek God's will for your life and your place in The Body of Christ and know that what God has created you to do is important and significant for advancing the Kingdom.

I find that sometimes people think they are not valuable or useful to the Kingdom of God. That's a lie. Never believe that you can't make a difference. One of the biggest lies that Satan tells people is that they can't make a difference. Yes you can!

Here's a few pointers for you.
- Keep your focus on God....
- Put God first in everything you do....
- Stay in the Word....
- Pray in the Spirit.....
- Worship Continuously.....

Do not engage with this spirit. You will become angry and harbor a murderous spirit, you will become a renegade, a vagabond, a wanderer, you will not be able to connect properly in the body of Christ.

God is preparing a way to usher in His Glory. Don't be deceived by the enemy. I pray that your eyes will be opened and enlightened, and that the Sound of Awakening will descend upon you and your region. Let us become kingdom minded and come together for a kingdom purpose: to open up the gates of our cities and nation so the King of Glory can come in. It is in His presence that our lives will be transformed into what He created us to be.

May every root of competition in you die right now. Let no seeds of jealousy, strife, rivalry, bitterness, or division rise up in us Lord. Kill every evil and vile work within our lives and within our hearts right now and fill us up with the fruit of the Spirit which is: love, joy, peace, patience, kindness, goodness, faithfulness, gentleness and self-control. May these rule and reign in all of us.

Day 15
God's Perfect Gift

Acts 2:38-39 (NLT) Peter replied, "Each of you must repent of your sins and turn to God, and be baptized in the name of Jesus Christ for the forgiveness of your sins. Then you will receive the gift of the Holy Spirit. This promise is to you, to your children, and to those far away —all who have been called by the Lord our God."

When Jesus was preparing to return to The Father in Heaven they had a plan to send the helper, who would be accessible to all believers. He would be a gift from The Father to His children, those who would believe and receive this perfect gift.

Let's start with this first; Holy Spirit is not an "It". Let's begin by referring to Him as a person. He is the third part of the Godhead. (Father, Son and Holy Ghost- or Holy Spirit)

The Holy Spirit is the best teacher we can have. He will lead you into all truth. He sanctifies, empowers, helps set us free, washes and cleanses us. He reveals the deeper things of God. He gives us wisdom and He speaks to, in and through us.

*John 14:26 (ESV) "But the **Helper**, the Holy Spirit, whom the Father will send in My name, He will **teach you all things**, and bring to your remembrance all that I said to you.*

Jesus told His disciples to wait for the promise of The Father, which was the gift of the Holy Spirit.

Act 1:4 (ESV) And while staying with them he ordered them not to depart from Jerusalem, but to wait for the promise of the Father, which, he said, "you heard from me; 5 for John baptized with water, but you will be baptized with the Holy Spirit not many days from now."

Act 1:8 (ESV) But you will receive power when the Holy Spirit has come upon you, and you will be my witnesses in Jerusalem and in all Judea and Samaria, and to the end of the earth.

What a joyful day It was when the tongues of fire descended upon that crowd in the upper room. These lives would never be the same, just as our lives should never be the same once we encounter the true fire of God.

Acts 2:3-4 (NLT) Then, what looked like flames or tongues of fire appeared and settled on each of them. And everyone present was filled with the Holy Spirit and began speaking in other languages, as the Holy Spirit gave them this ability.

The baptism of the Holy Spirit is a gift that we can receive along with Salvation. The moment we receive Jesus as our Lord and Savior, we can also receive the baptism of the Holy Spirit. This gift is evidenced by speaking in tongues or a heavenly language. Some people call it a prayer language or spirit language. It is also called the gifts of tongues. In the book of Acts, when the disciples gathered in the Upper Room, the Holy Spirit descended upon them and gave them the power to witness (Acts 1:8; 2:4). The gift of the Holy Spirit empowered them to fulfill their God given assignment and it will you too.

Even though I had been saved for years, My life was radically transformed when I received the baptism of the Holy Spirit. God revealed to me the importance of this and how it would empower me and give me the strength that I needed to stand strong through the storms. I didn't really have a clear understanding of it all so I searched out the scriptures and finally told God one night that if it was a true gift from Him, I knew it would be good because He was a good Father and that I wanted it. I stepped out in faith and received it and I have never looked back or doubted whether this was real or not. I didn't have to. It was evidenced by the change in my life. I had been marked by the Fire of God. I went from being a quiet, insecure person to one on fire for God. I loved sharing my testimony and my God encounters with others and seeing their lives transformed by the power of God.

It's a sure promise from God, available to all those who believe.

*Act 2:38 (ESV) And Peter said to them, "Repent, and be baptized every one of you in the name of Jesus Christ for the forgiveness of your sins; and **you will receive** the gift of the Holy Spirit.*

The Holy Spirit will give you the boldness to stand.

*Act 4:31 (ESV) And when they had prayed, the place in which they were gathered together was shaken, and they were all filled with the Holy Spirit and continued to speak the word of God with **boldness**.*

Here is what Jesus said when He was explaining the role of Holy Spirit to His disciples:

*John 16:13 (ESV) When the Spirit of truth comes, he will **guide you into all the truth,** for he will not speak on his own authority, but whatever he hears he will speak, and he will declare to you the things that are to come. 14 He will glorify me, for he will take what is mine and declare it to you.*

It's really amazing to think that Jesus gave to us **all** that The Father gave to Him and that we are joint heirs with Christ.

Rom 8:26 (ESV) In the same way the Spirit also helps our weakness; for we do not know how to pray as we should, but the Spirit Himself intercedes for us with groanings too deep for words;

The Holy Spirit strengthens us and also directly intercedes for us. How cool is that! When we pray in the Spirit, we are praying the perfect will of God. It was God's perfect plan so you could carry Jesus inside you. The Holy Spirit will lead you and guide you in all areas of your life. Ask God to baptize you with His Holy Spirit and Fire. It's a free gift, like salvation. Don't miss out on God's perfect gift to you.

This gift is the one that the devil has fought against the most because he knows the power that it holds. He knows that it will build up an understanding of spiritual matters within you. It will build you up like nothing else. It will mature you to the level that God wants you to be. It's a supernatural act of faith.

Jud 1:20 (ESV) But you, beloved, building yourselves up in your most holy faith and praying in the Holy Spirit,

Praying in the Holy Spirit will strengthen you and give you hope like no other.

Rom 15:13 (ESV) May the God of hope fill you with all joy and peace in believing, so that by the power of the Holy Spirit you may abound in hope.

Ask God right now to fill you with the Holy Spirit and fire. If you have been baptized in the Holy Spirit before, tell Him that you desire a fresh baptism of Holy Spirit and Fire. Lift your hands up and receive it. Now say, "Thank you Father for your gift of the Holy Spirit and I'm going to speak in tongues now." Then open your mouth and let it come from up and out of your belly. You have to put voice to it. You have to step out in faith and do it. Don't think about how it sounds or think it's silly, just receive and allow God to do what He wants to do. This gift is for every believer. It's a promise for you, your children and all generations to come. It's powerful. It's the one gift that you have to step out in faith and do something with to activate it and also it is the doorway to the other gifts of the spirit.

Act 2:39 (ESV) For the promise is for you and for your children and for all who are far off, everyone whom the Lord our God calls to himself.

Congratulations, now just be aware that Satan isn't happy about it because he knows the power that the Holy Spirit has and he will do his best to steal this gift from you. As a matter of fact, he may already be telling you that it's not real and how silly you must look and sound. Don't listen to him. He's a liar. Put your focus on God and continue to thank Him for this precious gift and now you can begin a new and fresh relationship with the Holy Spirit, the third person of the godhead that was there at creation and also there at Jesus's resurrection. He now lives inside of you!

Rom 8:11 (ESV) If the Spirit of him who raised Jesus from the dead dwells in you, he who raised Christ Jesus from the dead will also give life to your mortal bodies through his Spirit who dwells in you.

God, in all His wisdom, always knows what we will respond to. He baptized me in the Holy Spirit in my sleep one night and I sat up in the bed speaking in tongues. Nobody touched me or laid hands on me to receive. I was searching and asked God if it was really a gift from Him to please give it to me and I wanted it. Once I surrendered, He was able to work with that. God can always work with a surrendered heart.

Go ahead and surrender yours to Him now. He's a good Father and only gives good gifts to His children. It is His desire to baptize with His Fire and fill you with His Holy Spirit. Your life will never be the same.

Day 16
Jesus's Commission Was Simple... COME, And then GO....

As Jesus gathered his disciples, he said, *"COME and follow me and I will make you fishers of men."* He also said things like in *Matt 16:24 (ESV) He said, ..."If anyone would come after me, let him deny himself and take up his cross and follow me."*

Again, He revealed a portion of why He came in *Matt 10:34 (ESV) "Do not think that I have come to bring peace to the earth. I have not come to bring peace, but a sword." 1John 3:8b (ESV) The reason the Son of God appeared was to destroy the works of the devil.*

These are just a few of the reasons why Jesus, The Son of God, came to earth as a man.

Jesus said in *John 10:27 (ESV) "My sheep hear my voice, and I know them, and they follow me."* To be counted as one of His sheep, we must learn to hear the voice of God and then follow Him. When we hear those voices in our head, it's either the voice of God, the voice of the enemy (Satan or his demons) or it could just be our own fleshy self talking. We have to learn to discern the different voices and know which one to follow.

As Bible believing Christians, we are supposed to be imitators of Christ. Jesus came to show us the way to treat others and how He wanted us to affect the earth. We are to walk as a living example of Him; treating others as He would have treated them. Everyone who came to Jesus asking Him for help got their needs met, regardless of what it was. Some came for salvation, some for healing, some for deliverance. He was a true manifestation of Heaven on Earth. He came to demonstrate the Kingdom of Heaven on earth and so should we.

The disciples walked with Jesus for three and a half years. He trained them, He taught them, He equipped them. He prepared them to finish the work that He had begun. He expected them to pick up where He left off and continue in the same manner in which He had done. Jesus speaking in John 16:15 (AMP) said, "Everything that the Father has is Mine. That is what I meant when I said that He [the Spirit] will take the things that are Mine and will reveal (declare, disclose, transmit) it to you."

Our commission is the same today as it was then:
Matt 28:19-20 (ESV) **Go** *therefore and make disciples of all nations, baptizing them in the name of the Father and of the Son and of the Holy Spirit, teaching them to observe all that I have commanded you. And behold, I am with you always, to the end of the age.*

In Mark, He expounded on it:
*Mark 16:15-18 (ESV) And he said to them, "**Go** into all the world and proclaim the gospel to the whole creation. Whoever believes and is baptized will be saved, but whoever does not believe will be condemned. And these signs will accompany those who believe: in my name they will cast out demons; they will speak in new tongues; they will pick up serpents with their hands; and if they drink any deadly poison, it will not hurt them; they will lay their hands on the sick, and they will recover."*

So COME to Christ, give your heart and life to Him, cast all your cares on Him, learn His ways and become an imitator of Him and a demonstrator of the Kingdom of God. Then GO and teach others to do the same. We were never called to be pew warmers or "Sunday only Christians", but to live a *lifestyle* of Christ reflected in us.

I'll sum it up with this: *1Cor 4:20 (ESV) For the kingdom of God does not consist in talk but in power.*

Come to Christ and then Go and preach and teach the Kingdom of God and affect the earth! You can do this Child of God. You must rise up in the power and authority that Christ has given you. You are much more than just a sinner, saved by grace. You are also a mighty warrior forged in the furnace of affliction and the fire of God; formed and fashioned by the very hand of the Almighty God.

Isa 48:10 (ESV) Behold, I have refined you, but not as silver; I have tried you in the furnace of affliction.

Everything that you have gone through, every heartbreak, every loss, every tear will be used by God to destroy the works of Satan. Don't let any of it go to waste. Allow God to heal you and set you free and when He does the enemy will have no hold on you any longer.

Day 17
Be Holy You Vessel of Honor

1Pe 1:16 (KJV) Because it is written, Be ye holy; for I am holy.

God wants us to come into that place of total surrender with Him where He can save us, heal us, deliver us and make us to be like Him.

Heb 12:14 (KJV) Strive to live in peace with everybody and pursue that consecration and holiness without which no one will [ever] see the Lord.

Holiness is total devotion to God, consecrated to His service, being of one mind with God, set apart from ordinary purposes, dedicated to the Lord, separated for a holy purpose.

2Ti 2:20 (ESV) Now in a great house there are not only vessels of gold and silver but also of wood and clay, some for honorable use, some for dishonorable. 21 Therefore, if anyone cleanses himself from what is dishonorable, he will be a vessel for honorable use, set apart as holy, useful to the master of the house, ready for every good work.

A Holy person will strive to be like God everyday. They will be totally endeavored to turn away from every known sin and to know everything about the one they serve. They will have a desire to please Him and do His will and have an even greater fear of displeasing or disobeying Him.

Holiness is being of one mind with God. It is coming into agreement with God in all areas of your life. That means we hate what He hates and we love what He loves, and we measure everything in this world by the standard of His Word.

The Word tells us to be an imitator of Christ, to do what He did. We are to strive for holiness. God's spirit lives in us, so we have to learn to take care of our temple, for God's temple is holy.

1Co 3:16-17 (ESV) Do you not know that you are God's temple and that God's Spirit dwells in you? If anyone destroys God's temple, God will destroy him. For God's temple is holy, and you are that temple.

1Co 6:19-20 (ESV) Or do you not know that your body is a temple of the Holy Spirit within you, whom you have from God? You are not your own, for you were bought with a price. So glorify God in your body.

1Pe 2:9 (ESV) But you are a chosen race, a royal priesthood, a holy nation, a people for his own possession, that you may proclaim the excellencies of him who called you out of darkness into his marvelous light.

Jesus paid the price. It was paid in full at the cross when He declared, " It is finished." His blood that was shed is sufficient for all of your needs. Whether you need salvation, healing, deliverance, forgiveness or provisions, His blood covered it all.

It's time for you to come to the foot of the cross and ask him for whatever it is that you need. Surrender yourself to him, repent of any wrongdoing and ask for forgiveness and let Him begin a work in you to make you Holy before Him.

Rom 12:1 (ESV) I appeal to you therefore, brothers, by the mercies of God, to present your bodies as a living sacrifice, holy and acceptable to God, which is your spiritual worship.

God is coming back for a bride. A pure and holy one without spot or blemish or wrinkle. We must be ready. We start by positioning our heart in His hands.

Eph 5:27 (ESV) So that He might present the church to Himself in splendor, without spot or wrinkle or any such thing, that She might be holy and without blemish.

He's waiting and looking for those so committed to Him that they are willing to lay it all down and turn from all the things that have distracted them or held them hostage or kept them in bondage. Where is God's Bride? Where is this perfect surrendered Church that God is looking for? It's time to let go and Let God bring her forth in His power and might!

We have to die to self before we can live for Christ. It's not easy. There's a huge price to pay, but the benefits are out of this world and it pays big dividends! We have to learn to lay it all down. Lay it all down on the altar and then ask God what is still in us that needs to go? Everything that you are holding onto becomes an idol and He is a jealous God. He wants you all to himself. He wants to remove those false idols. He wants you to get to that place where it's just you and Him. Then He will direct your path and you will gladly follow.

Why not let today be that day that you surrender everything to Him? Then allow Him to resurrect those areas of your life that have died or need help. It's a process of trusting God with your life, your family, your finances, your destiny, everything you have.

As you surrender your life to Him, you will find the strength to overcome. The power to overcome is found in submitting and surrendering everything to Him. Once you do, your life will never be the same! Just say, " Lord, I give it all to you. I fully surrender my life to you and I want to live the rest of my life for you. Make me a vessel honorable for your service and useful for your kingdom."

Gal 2:20 (ESV) I have been crucified with Christ. It is no longer I who live, but Christ who lives in me. And the life I now live in the flesh I live by faith in the Son of God, who loved me and gave himself for me.

Just surrender your heart to Him and say, "I am yours and you, my Lord, are mine. I will praise you with everything within me. Have your way in me."

Day 18
What Are You Sowing?

Galatians 6:7 (NLT) Don't be misled—you cannot mock the justice of God. You will always harvest what you plant.

Regardless of what seed you plant, you will get a crop unless the enemy comes in and steals it. What size crop depends on several factors. The seed must be good and it must be placed in good ground and it needs the proper nutrients and care. In the natural, if you plant tomato seeds you get tomatoes, if you plant corn seeds, you get corn. In the spirit realm you also get what you plant. If you sow contention and strife, that's what you will get. If you sow kindness and goodness that too will reproduce.

In the spirit realm, our portion is to plant the seed. The Holy Spirit takes it from there and produces the harvest. The law of sowing and reaping says that " You will reap what you sow. " This means that whether you sow good seeds or bad seeds, you will reap a harvest. In other words, if you Sow love, you will get love. If you Sow anger, you will get anger. It's the law of sowing and reaping.

We should all be working and desiring to produce the fruits of the Spirit as described in Galatians.

Galatians 5:22-23 (NLT) But the Holy Spirit produces this kind of fruit in our lives: love, joy, peace, patience, kindness, goodness, faithfulness, gentleness, and self-control. There is no law against these things!

The Bible doesn't say, You will know them by their gifting or by their talents or by what they say. It says you will know them by their fruits. *(Mat 7:20)* This is how we can tell if someone is truly surrendered to God.

We have the honor and privilege to be able to walk with The Holy Spirit and allow Him to birth some great fruit in us for the Glory of God. However, if these fruits are not evident in our lives, it could be that they have not been sown in good ground or they may not have reached maturity yet. They may still require proper nutrients, such as understanding or discipleship to bring forth the great harvest.

Just because your fruit is still in seed form doesn't mean the harvest isn't coming. Some seeds lie dormant for years. Some have to be scarified before they will germinate. If they are too hard, they have to be cut, pierced or broken in order to allow what's inside to come out. Jesus's body was broken for us and His blood poured out.

Don't give up on your harvest while it's still in seed form. This is when most people grow weary. This is the time to hang on to your promise and believe God for it to come forth in His timing and His way.

If you have sown the good seed of the Holy Spirit in your life, know that it's in there germinating and it will come forth as God designed it too. Some things take more time and can only grow in deep dark places.

A seed will never reach its full potential until it is placed alone in the dark, covered with soil and buried. That seed will miraculously push its way through the darkness into the light.

When you go through hard times, God isn't burying you to stay there in the darkness, He's planting you so you can produce some rare exotic fruit that can only be produced in that deep, dark, intimate place by the crushing and the scarring and the dying to self.

Don't let the enemy convince you there's no harvest coming! Sow your seeds and leave the rest up to God. It takes faith. We have to plant it and then let it be. We can't go dig up our seed everyday in the natural to see if it's sprouted yet. So don't do it in the spiritual either.

Believe it and decree it! Say, "I planted good seed!! My harvest is coming!! Thank you Father for my harvest."

*Galatians 6:8-10 (NLT) 8 Those who live only to satisfy their own sinful nature will harvest decay and death from that sinful nature. But those who live to please the Spirit will harvest everlasting life from the Spirit. 9 So let's not get tired of doing what is good. **At just the right time we will reap a harvest of blessing if we don't give up.** 10 Therefore, whenever we have the opportunity, we should do good to everyone—especially to those in the family of faith.*

With the Holy Spirit Living inside us and guiding us, we all possess the capability to produce a bumper crop. Did you know that the Fruits of the Spirit of His goodness are inside you? Release your seed wherever you go. Give away love, joy, peace, patience, kindness, goodness, faithfulness, gentleness, and self-control to all those you meet and watch the harvest come.

Mar 4:20 (TM) But the seed planted in the good earth represents those who hear the Word, embrace it, and produce a harvest beyond their wildest dreams.

Day 19
Conquer or Be Conquered

Joshua 1:2-3 (NLT) Moses my servant is dead. Therefore, the time has come for you to lead these people, the Israelites, across the Jordan River into the land I am giving them. I promise you what I promised Moses: 'Wherever you set foot, you will be on land I have given you...

Joshua was raised up to take the Israelites into the Promised Land. God had already said that it was to be theirs and they were to go in and take the land. It was part of their inheritance. The only problem was that the people with him focused on the giants, not the fruit. They did not have the faith to step into their destiny, like Joshua and Caleb did and the entire nation suffered for it and because of their unbelief, they wandered in the wilderness for forty years.(Numbers 13)

It's the same way with us today. It's hard when everyone around you is doing the opposite of what you feel like God is telling you to do. Any faith you have gets wiped out by fear and doubt. Then the giants come to consume you. The giants you are facing that are trying to steal your destiny or thwart your life purpose might be fear, intimidation, rejection, unforgiveness, offense, shame or jealousy. If you carry these through life, you will make poor decisions, use bad judgement and do things to your body that destroy you.

You won't consider yourself worthy enough to receive the blessings from The Lord and you will try to sabotage your own success and fulfillment in life. This can be done willingly or subconsciously. But you can rise up out of the ashes of your bad choices and mishaps and begin a new life in Christ. God is always there with open arms waiting for your return and to restore you and make you whole.

There is no sin or transgression that is so terrible that He can't forgive; or no place that you are in that is so low that He can't lift you up out of it. He wants to wipe away every tear, along with all the shame and heartbreak and set you on a new path to your God-given destiny today.

Take a few minutes and consider your life. Go back to those abandoned and almost forgotten dreams that you used to cherish. God can resurrect them. They can still come to pass. God wants to give you the desires of your heart. He put them there in the first place and He wants you to live an abundant life full of peace and joy.

Psa 37:4 (ESV) Delight yourself in the LORD, and he will give you the desires of your heart.

Where is your toughest battle? The place that God wants to bless you is the area that the enemy fights you the hardest. You have to rise up and take a stand and push back the darkness with the light of Christ. The enemy comes to devour you and he has no sympathy or mercy on you. His job is to steal, kill and destroy every good thing that God has promised you.

Don't give in to the enemy and his lies. There is hope for you and for this nation as well. If the people of God, will arise with the spirit of Joshua and Caleb, and take their place in the Kingdom of God. As they come together in unity with God and the body of Christ, (the Ekklesia) they will take back what the enemy has stolen and there will be victory in your life and in this nation.

Psalms 18:3 (NLT) I called on the Lord, who is worthy of praise, and he saved me from my enemies.

Life has its challenges. Some days you feel defeated as though the hounds of hell have been unleashed against you and your destiny; and I hate to tell you, but they have. Satan knows his time is short and he's holding nothing back. But I'm here to tell you that I know how defeated you feel as Satan keeps pounding on you. But, there's good news. God is on your side. This is a test and you are going to pass. You are actually doing better than you think you are. God says to you today, "Arise and shine my love, you are doing better than you think. Step out in the boldness and in the authority that I have given you and I will back you up. You got this."

Psalms 18:29-35 (NLT) In your strength I can crush an army; with my God I can scale any wall. God's way is perfect. All the Lord's promises prove true. He is a shield for all who look to him for protection. For who is God except the Lord? Who but our God is a solid rock? God arms me with strength, and he makes my way perfect. He makes me as surefooted as a deer, enabling me to stand on mountain heights. He trains my hands for battle; he strengthens my arm to draw a bronze bow. You have given me your shield of victory. Your right hand supports me; your help has made me great.

Throw your fears away. God has this and He has you. There is nothing you can't do, with His help!

Day 20
The Battle Is Still Over Who You Will Worship

There was a decree that went out across the land. The law had been established. When the music starts, you bow to the golden image or you will be thrown in the fiery furnace. The king was saying, you have a choice; bow to me or burn for Him.

It says in *Dan 3:6 (ESV) And whoever does not fall down and worship shall immediately be cast into a burning fiery furnace.*

The enemy always threatens you. He works off of fear and Intimidation. He's a bully.

Satan still wants the world to bow down and worship him. He tried to get Jesus to worship him while tempting Him in the wilderness and he will do the same to you. He desires worship, he was the lead worshipper in heaven and was created for worship. He and his entire choir were kicked out of Heaven for treason. He attempted to overthrow God and take His throne. (How dumb and rebellious that was) That's why we have the battle over worship. The enemy knows worship is about who you serve and who you are loyal to.

In verse 15, King Nebuchadnezzar gives them one more chance to bow to his evil schemes. Then he makes a mockery out of God and brings his own greatness into the equation when he asks the question, "who is the god who will deliver you out of my hands?"

Mockery, Pride, Ego.... There's a "Who is stronger and better than me" Attitude....

Dan 3:16-18 (ESV) Shadrach, Meshach, and Abednego answered and said to the king, "O Nebuchadnezzar, we have no need to answer you in this matter. 17 If this be so, our God whom we serve is able to deliver us from the burning fiery furnace, and he will deliver us out of your hand, O king. 18 But if not, be it known to you, O king, that we will NOT serve your gods or worship the golden image that you have set up."

When the enemy accuses you, don't give into his lies and schemes and false accusations. Don't bow to him and his tactics. Keep your focus on God and His goodness. God always provides a way of escape. If you stay true to Him and His call, He will take care of you. Just continue on the path that He has placed you on and determine in your heart that you will persevere in the things that He has called you to do, knowing that He will never leave you.

I love their response to the King. They were certain that their God was well able to deliver them, but if He didn't, for whatever reason, that was Ok too. They had complete trust in God. They refused to bow to the false idol, regardless of the outcome. They knew that they were to have NO other Gods but the true and Living God.

God is looking for those who, like the 3 Hebrews, are sold out to Him and will follow Him fully and completely regardless of the outcome. He's looking for those who will say, regardless of what happens, I know God you are able to do all things. I know you are the King of Kings and Lord of Lords. I know that you are good and I will serve you and follow you whether I am on top of the mountain or down in the valley. Those who will say, whether you deliver me or I perish, I will still praise you and speak of your goodness Lord! Though you slay me, I will trust you God.

Worship is not just about singing a nice song or playing a musical instrument. It's about a surrendered lifestyle, one totally surrendered to God. Worship is about who you serve. Choose for yourself this day whom you will serve and stand strong with no backing down.

Day 21
Barrenness Can Birth Greatness

Luke 1:36 (ESV) And behold, your relative Elizabeth in her old age has also conceived a son, and this is the sixth month with her who was called barren. 37 For nothing will be impossible with God.

There have been a lot of great people birthed from barren women. Women who refused to give up; those who refused to take no for an answer. Lots of greatness comes from barren places and barren people who refuse to give in to the lies of the enemy; people who refuse to bow to Baal or refuse to eat the king's meat or those who refuse to party with the wicked king.

Elizabeth remained in her house for 5 months. (Luke 1:24) She was preparing herself and her mind and seeking God and pressing into Him for what He was doing in her life. When God is birthing something through you, there's going to be a time of barrenness followed by a time of consecration and a time of preparation.

When God is trying to birth something great in the earth, He will make you barren for a season, to make you so desperate and hungry for Him that what you bring forth and what you birth is a supernatural seed that has been pressed and squeezed out of the very hand of God. He will take you to a place of humility where in the natural, you don't desire to go, but in the spiritual you will crave to be there, because His presence is there. Answers are there. Comfort is there.

God told Abraham (Gen 12) to go away from his country, his relatives and his father's house (to leave everything that was familiar to him) and go to a new land, a new place where he would have to start over and build from the ground up with a new foundation. He would be totally dependent upon God. Then God would make him a great nation, make his name great and bless those who bless him.

Genesis 12:1-3 (NLT) The Lord had said to Abram, "Leave your native country, your relatives, and your father's family, and go to the land that I will show you. I will make you into a great nation. I will bless you and make you famous, and you will be a blessing to others. I will bless those who bless you and curse those who treat you with contempt. All the families on earth will be blessed through you."

Sometimes God chooses to tear everything down and start over with a new firm foundation built on prayer, truth and the Word. In life, sometimes we develop faulty foundations and unstable beliefs based on traditions, worldly values and even our own personal agenda or fleshly desires rather than the solid truth and the Word of God. We must learn to follow God, being fully surrendered to Him and His will. My life verse through my barren time became "Thou He slay me, I will trust Him."(Job 13:15)

You may not understand it when God calls you. You may be afraid to step out in faith. You may have to separate yourself from the negative people that have been around you and get in a barren place where God can fertilize your seed and water it. It is in this time of barrenness that great things are birthed. It is in the wilderness that your emotions are stabilized, wounds are healed and you give it all to God. It is in this time of difficulty that your priorities shift and change, all arrogance, ego and pride will slowly melt away and a spirit of humility will rise up. It is a time when your heart is laid bare and naked before God and He refashions it and forms you a new heart; One like His.

It is not easy. It is very costly. It will cost you everything. Is it worth it? Absolutely! Ask God to use your life, to prepare you in whatever manner He sees fit, to equip you to do His work and then step back, surrender yourself, your will and your ways and allow Him to do what He wants to do.

There is greatness inside you. That seed that God placed in you already holds the DNA of what He created you to be. Just like the acorn already holds the capacity to be a mighty oak tree, you already have everything inside you to be who God created you to be. It just needs to be put in the right environment to be cultivated and nourished and allowed to grow to full term.

Don't allow the enemy to steal your seed. He's a liar and he wants to keep you pressed down and silent. The enemy has unleashed a spirit of acquiescence over the land, where we just go along with whatever we are told and blindly follow the media and deceived leaders to destruction. We've been lulled to sleep by a spirit of complacency. We've been told that we can't speak the truth, or it's not nice or "Christian-like" to speak up. It's a lie. Don't be deceived. It's all Satan's plan to steal or kill you and your seed. He knows that what you carry inside of you is valuable and needed for the Kingdom of God. He knows that if your seed is birthed, it will wreak havoc on the kingdom of darkness! Your seed needs to be birthed!

The enemy may have told you that you can't make a difference, you are not good enough or that God can't use you because of your past or your shortcomings. He's a liar. Don't fall for it. Your life matters! Your seed matters and needs to be birthed! You have a purpose! Let God mold you into the person that He created you to be. Come to the cross, to the feet of Jesus and pour yourself out to Him today and allow Him to fill you up with His love!

Day 22
The Power of His Love

John 3:16 (ESV) For God so loved the world, that he gave his only Son, that whoever believes in him should not perish but have eternal life.

God's love never fails. It's not like the earthly love of a man or woman. It's so much more than that. God loves us so much that He calls us His children. He sent His only Son to die for us. That is true love.

Jesus left all of Heaven to come down here to earth and be mocked, ridiculed and tortured so we could have eternal life. He took what we deserved (death) , so we could have what He deserved. (eternal life)

You will never look in the eyes of someone that God didn't love enough to die for.

God is pouring out His love upon His people right now. He is looking for those who are open to receive it. He has so much that He wants to impart to the Body of Christ right now for this next move of God that is coming upon the earth. It's going to be a demonstration of His power and His love for all to see. God is looking for men and women of covenant, that He can partner with to usher in the Glory of God to the world.

Abraham entered into a covenant with God and God promised him that he would make him the Father of many nations. At that time, Abraham had no children of his own and he was old and it looked impossible for that to come to pass in the natural. Some of you today, don't look like what God has called you to be either. Your promise hasn't come to pass and it doesn't look like there is any way that it can. It just looks impossible. But nothing is impossible with God.

Luke 1:37 For nothing will be impossible with God."

God is saying for you to trust Him and step out on what faith you have. Believe that somehow and some way, God will bring it to pass. Don't give in to the lies of the enemy and allow him to kill your dreams and steal your promises and don't birth an Ishmael by stepping out of God's will and timing and trying to make it happen on your own. Walking in love is learning to trust in what you can't see and feel, but believing it will come to pass just because God said so.

Jesus loves us just as the Father loves us. Everything that God gave to Jesus, He took it and gave it to us. (John 16:15)

The Word says that there is no greater love than to lay down your life for your friends and we show that we are His friends by doing what he says to do.

John 15:13-14 (ESV) Greater love has no one than this, that someone lay down his life for his friends. 14 You are my friends if you do what I command you.

Let God saturate you in His love today and pour it out upon you to overflowing. His perfect Love will change your heart, bring healing to old places and cast out your fears, for perfect love casts out all fears. (1 John 4:18) Then you can pour it out to others and see lives changed by the transforming power of God's love. Love is a mighty weapon that will take down giants and heal nations.

1Jn 4:16 (ESV) So we have come to know and to believe the love that God has for us. God is love, and whoever abides in love abides in God, and God abides in him.

Day 23
Make The Devil Pay

The devil comes to torment you and when you allow him in, he will do just that. He is a bully and he will push his way in any way that he can. When he finds an open door, he barrels through it. The Holy Spirit is a perfect gentleman. He stands at the door and knocks.

Every trial that you have been through has a purpose. Everything that was meant for evil, God can use it for good. That very thing that you went through, it was so horrible that you thought it would kill you. But it didn't. The enemy tried, but he did not succeed. Let that very thing that was meant to destroy you, strengthen you and empower you and then you can testify to others about the goodness of God through the battles and the storms. Your overcoming testimony will bring hope and healing to others.

When hard times come, tell the Devil that you will not quit and this attack will only make you stronger. Pray hard and pray long. Pray loud enough to scare the dogs and make them hide under the bed. These are some of your weapons of warfare:

- His Presence
- Worship
- Dance
- Prayer
- Praying in the Spirit

- Fasting
- Giving
- Proclaiming the Word
- Decreeing His promises
- Honoring Others

Don't give in to Satan's lies. He comes to take you out and to devour that seed that is inside of you. He wants to see you miserable and broken. He doesn't play fair and his motives are evil and he wants you to turn your back on God and walk away. Don't do it. You have destiny and purpose.

I know life can be hard. There are some seasons that are full of tragedy and pain and you feel as though you won't survive. But you will. Go ahead and cry your tears if you need to. Then pull yourself up by your bootstraps (as we say in the south) and shake yourself off. Rise up in the power and strength that God has given you. Learn to let your struggles make you stronger than before and even more determined to finish your race and complete your God-given assignment.

You want to get back at the devil for what he's done to you? Then don't quit, be determined to finish your race and endure to the end. Go ahead and become everything that God has created you to be and nothing that Satan says you are. We can't really make Satan have a nervous breakdown, but we can stand up against him in the power of the Holy Spirit that lives inside of us (Rom. 8:11) and not bow to his wickedness. You can be victorious over Satan. God has given you that authority. Rise up, Child of God. You are not defeated. You are a finisher and The Finisher lives on the inside of you.

Luke 10:19 (KJV) Behold, I give unto you power to tread on serpents and scorpions, and over all the power of the enemy: and nothing shall by any means hurt you.

Walk in the power and authority that He has given you and you will do some damage to the Kingdom of darkness!

Day 24
Rend The Heavens

Today the Father is looking for His end-time remnant; His Bride, a people who will be led by His voice and His Word. He's looking for those who will surrender to Him and obey Him fully. Man has been looking for great signs and wonders, while God is looking for a willing heart of obedience. The true remnant of this generation will hear His voice and obey despite ridicule, persecution and judgment. They will not forsake God nor will they compromise His way. They will not promote God's Glory or market it for themselves. Instead, they will be good stewards of the eternal flame that God has entrusted unto them and they will be led by the Holy Spirit. This end-time remnant will be obedient and follow God as they did in the wilderness with the cloud and the fire. (Exodus 13:21)

He is looking for those who will surrender their hearts and lives fully to Him. Like a good Father, He is always calling us back to Him.

Joel 2:12 (ESV) "Yet even now," declares the LORD, "return to me with all your heart, with fasting, with weeping, and with mourning; 13 and rend your hearts and not your garments." Return to the LORD your God, for he is gracious and merciful, slow to anger, and abounding in steadfast love; and he relents over disaster.

He is looking to activate the intercessors and the watchmen and those who will cry out to Him for His presence to come down, invade the earth and dwell amongst us. He is searching for those true worshippers who will worship Him in Spirit and in Truth. (John 4-23-24)

Isa 64:1 (ESV) Oh that you would rend the heavens and come down, that the mountains might quake at your presence— 2 as when fire kindles brushwood and the fire causes water to boil— to make your name known to your adversaries, and that the nations might tremble at your presence!

There's a shaking going on in the body of Christ. Everything that can be shaken will be shaken. Some will be shaken in and others will be shaken out. God is causing a Holy separation to take place. He is establishing a Kingdom that is built on a solid foundation of Jesus Christ that cannot be shaken.

Heb 12:28 (ESV) Therefore let us be grateful for receiving a kingdom that cannot be shaken, and thus let us offer to God acceptable worship, with reverence and awe, 29 for our God is a consuming fire.

I pray that the people of God will come into Unity with the Father, Son and Holy Spirit. That they will rise up, get healed, equipped and take their place in the Kingdom of God. I say Let the Son set you free and you will be free indeed! I call forth the Army of God to Arise! May the Sons and Daughters of the Living God know their identity and authority and walk in it. May they throw down their traditions and man made religions and false identities and become a new creation as promised in the Word. (2 Cor 5:17)

May we only bow to the Lord Jesus Christ and Him alone. Jesus is coming back for His Bride perfected, without spot, wrinkle or blemish. I say let the Warrior Bride Emerge and Arise and Become all that God created her to be! It's time to take a stand now between Heaven and Earth and watch God's righteousness reign down!

2 Chr 7:14 says, "If MY people"... It doesn't say "If the world." People of God, if you will humble yourself, repent and cry out to God, He will hear your prayers and heal our land. What are you waiting for? It starts with YOU and ME. I will if you will. After all, Jesus said If any two agree.... I agree! How about you?

Mat 18:19 (ESV) Again I say to you, if two of you agree on earth about anything they ask, it will be done for them by my Father in heaven.

Let's pray together:
Father, We come into agreement together right now and repent for allowing such atrocities to take place on our land and to defile our nation. We seek your face and ask for your forgiveness and we agree together, as your children and your agents of the Kingdom of God-on Earth, to stand for truth and righteousness and use Your Word as our guide as long as we remain here on earth. Bring healing to our nation, Lord. Let it truly be One Nation Under God again.

Day 25
You Have Great Purpose

What is your purpose here on earth? **What will history say about you? What will heaven say?** If you could look ahead, 10, 20 or even 100 years from now, if the Lord tarries, what will the history books record about your life? Did you make a difference? Did you represent the Father to the world? Or did your life help build the kingdom of darkness?
Let that soak in a minute…. Selah…..

Will your life prove God right and the devil wrong? Will you make a difference on the earth? You are not here by chance. Your answers to these questions will determine how you will live the rest of your life. This is your moment; when you meet your destiny: Face to Face.

The world may call you an outcast or a misfit and reject you. You may have even been rejected by your parents or family or society. So what? Look at the life of John the Baptist. He was a little strange by the world's standard. People rejected him. But God created him to be like that- an evangelistic forerunner! He had a specific assignment from God and he lived it to the fullest. So can you! There are a lot of "odd" ones in the Bible. God didn't call you to blend in, He called you to stand out!

It doesn't matter how far you've strayed or how much you've sinned. When you come before God and lay it all at the foot of the

107

cross and ask God to forgive you and cleanse you and you receive Him as your savior, your past doesn't matter anymore. You are a new creation. *He calls you His beloved.*

2Co 5:17 (ESV) Therefore, if anyone is in Christ, he is a new creation. The old has passed away; behold, the new has come.

When we come and kneel at the foot of the cross, we are all equal at that point. God gives us all a fresh new start right there. But what we do after that very moment, determines our destiny. We have a choice; to fulfill our destiny or live a mediocre life.

God wants the very best for you. His plan is always redemption. Not condemnation. He is always there to pick you up out of the muck and set you on a rock.

Rom. 9: 25-26 (TM) I'll call nobodies and make them somebodies ; I'll call the unloved and make them beloved. In the place where they yelled out, "You're nobody!" they're calling you God's living children."

This is what He does best! He takes the broken and mends them. He takes the sick and makes them well. He takes the weary and makes them strong.

God is calling you out. He's looking for those who are sold out to Him. A Holy people, a Royal priesthood, a Holy nation; Those who will be bold and courageous for Him.

God is not looking for the religious leaders, He's looking for the humble, lovers of Him. Those who prefer His presence over their platform; Those who prefer the secret place over the spotlight; Those who prefer God's Glory over their own Glory.

God is looking for those who will give Him everything they have, So He can give them everything He has.

The apostle Paul said, "So too, at the present time there is a remnant chosen by grace" (Rom. 11: 5, NIV).

You are not a mistake. You have purpose. You have destiny. You may have been through some stuff, so what. That stuff doesn't define who you are. **Let your battle scars of the past become road maps to the future!**

You weren't called to live a mediocre life, to just live and die. There is so much more to life than that. You have great purpose! You were called to shake cities! You were called to affect nations! You were called to awaken a generation! You were called to be a history maker! Surrender it all to God and allow Him to take you to a place of healing so you can become all that He has created you to be! People are waiting for you to step into your destiny. All of creation is waiting for you to fully manifest into who God created you to be. You can do this.

Day 26
Life on the Threshing Floor

There will be trials and tests and struggles along your way to discover your destiny and to fulfill your walk with God. False grace, or the deceptive nature of grace will tell you that if you are following God and in His will that you will not have troubles. That is absolutely not true. Look what Jesus went through and He had no sin.

Everyone who chooses to follow Christ will have a threshing floor experience. It is a time of sifting and separating the good from the bad; when God is dealing with your stuff and wants you to surrender ALL of it to Him. You will feel like you can't go on and the things you have carried will become heavier and heavier. You must let go and let God bend you, break you, shape you and sift you like wheat. Your heart will feel as though it's going to explode from the pain, but it won't, as long as you stay surrendered to God.

Just look at the examples in the Bible. Over and over again those following God were tested. When we are following God, He doesn't always stop the trials but He does give us the grace to walk it out. He uses the trials to strengthen us and equip us for the work that He has called us to do. It's during those hard times that we grow closer to the Lord.

Listen to what the Apostle Paul said:

2Co 6:4 (NIV) Instead, in every way we demonstrate that we are God's servants by tremendous endurance in the midst of difficulties, hardships, and calamities; 5 in beatings, imprisonments, and riots; in hard work, sleepless nights, and hunger;

Jesus endured great sufferings and He had no sin; Abraham had to be willing to plunge the knife in his only son that he had waited years for; Paul was beaten, thrown in prison and left for dead more than once; Job was tested on all fronts including family, friends, wealth and health; David had to serve under a mad king who continuously hunted him down like an animal; Mary, the mother of Jesus, had to endure the shame and humiliation of being unwed and with child during a time when the punishment was stoning. Daniel was thrown in the lion's den. Joseph was falsely accused and thrown in the dungeon. As you see here, you are not alone. You are in good company.

Look what Jesus told Peter;
*Luke 22:31 (ESV) "Simon, Simon, behold, Satan demanded to have you, that he might **sift you like wheat,** 32 but I have prayed for you that your faith may not fail. And when you have turned again, strengthen your brothers."*

Jesus didn't tell Peter that it wouldn't happen. He told him that He prayed for him that his faith wouldn't fail him. The struggles and trials are a test of your faith; Will you continue to serve God and stand for Him when your life is not going so well? When things don't turn out like you planned? When loved ones die and sickness comes to you? Will you still love God if He chooses not to do things like you want?

There are so many people right now going through some of the hardest times they have ever known. Things that they have built a lifetime around have been snatched from them and they don't understand why.

In this fallen world that we live in, Satan comes to steal, kill and destroy. (John 10:10) He is a destroyer and a deceiver. He wants to see you beat down, addicted, brokenhearted, oppressed and sick. But praise God, Jesus came to set us free!!

Regardless of your circumstances, God is always the same. He loves you and wants the best for you. Continue to stand firm on the Word of God, even when you don't see what you are believing for happening yet. Put all your trust in Him and know that He is there for you. He will never leave you or forsake (abandon) you.

Day 27
A Circumcised Heart

Eze 36:26 (ESV) And I will give you a new heart, and a new spirit I will put within you. And I will remove the heart of stone from your flesh and give you a heart of flesh.

When we first come to God, we have some wrong thinking and fleshly desires but as we mature in the Lord and allow God to rule and reign over our lives and our emotions, we will be transformed. Our desires and ways will change. Those things we used to like, we will no longer hold close and those worldly things we used to love will no longer bring us pleasure. Our main desire will be to please God.

There is a maturing process we must go through and as we do, God will supernaturally change our hearts and our minds. As we surrender our hearts to God and allow Him to lead us, our lives will radically change. We won't be led by our emotions or feelings and the Word of God will be our guide in all things.

We are emotional beings. God created us to be that way. However, until we mature and fully turn our lives over to God and get healed, we can't trust our emotions to lead us correctly most of the time.

Jer 17:9 (ISV) The heart is more deceitful than anything. It is incurable—who can know it? 10 I am the LORD who searches the heart, who tests the inner depths to give to each person according to what he deserves, according to the fruit of his deeds.

David's desire was to follow God and do His will. He wasn't perfect and made some serious mistakes along the way, but his heart was tender to the things of God. It was his desire to do God's will. It was that position of his heart that made him a man after God's heart. ***How you position your heart toward God will determine How God positions His heart toward you.***

Psa 51:10 (ESV) Create in me a clean heart, O God, and renew a right spirit within me.

The Bible talks about circumcision of the heart, which is a process where we allow God to come in and cut away the fleshly parts which leaves a pure heart that is set aside to serve the Lord and Him only. It is a process where we are separated unto God and fully surrendered to Him for His good work.

Uncircumcised in heart would refer to being rebellious and not allowing God to lead you or come into your life in a real way. It would mean that you are resisting the leading of the Holy Spirit and God is not pleased with those actions.

Acts 7:51 (ESV) You stiff-necked people, uncircumcised in heart and ears, you always resist the Holy Spirit. As your fathers did, so do you.

It's a process of surrender; laying your heart open before the Lord and allowing Him to cut it, touch it, shape it, mold it, heal it and position it towards the things of God that He wants you to see and do. It's a time to seek God and say, "Lord, whatever is on your heart, put me right there in the middle of it." It is not a place of comfort, but a place of crushing. But the crushing won't kill you. If you surrender fully to Him, It will produce a sweet new wine that will make your heart pliable and tender to the things of God.

You may walk away with a limp, but your heart will have a new love, peace and joy for the things of God and you will never be the same! Praise God! Aren't you glad that God loves you enough to not allow you to stay the same? It is His desire to see you walking in the fullness of what He has for you! Get ready for the journey of your life!

Day 28
A False Gospel of Self

Luke 9:23 (ESV) And he said to all, "If anyone would come after me, let him deny himself and take up his cross daily and follow me."

There is a false gospel of "self". It's where you put yourself at the center of your focus and it lifts yourself up to a point that you become your own god. (which is no god at all) We live in a world that is very narcissistic, where people only care about themselves and will do whatever they want to get what they need to satisfy their own selfish, fleshly desires. The New Age movement operates under this spirit.

The true gospel is all about Jesus Christ and centered on Him and the Kingdom of God. The Word of God says we die to self. It teaches, *"He must increase, but I must decrease." (John 3:30 ESV)* God wants us to follow Him, not the world or ourselves.

Gal 2:20 (ESV) I have been crucified with Christ. It is no longer I who live, but Christ who lives in me. And the life I now live in the flesh I live by faith in the Son of God, who loved me and gave himself for me.

Satan always wants to glorify himself. He had an "I"problem. He exalted himself above God and above all creation. He thought more highly of himself than he was.

Isa 14:13 (ESV) You (Satan) said in your heart, 'I will ascend to heaven; above the stars of God I will set my throne on high; I will sit on the mount of assembly in the far reaches of the north; 14 I will ascend above the heights of the clouds; I will make myself like the Most High.'

(I must say that was a pretty dumb move, Satan.- Trying to overthrow God's throne? Really?)

The true gospel teaches us to surrender ourselves to God and put Him first in everything we do. It talks about laying down our lives and our agenda and picking up His. We must surrender to Him and allow Him to mold us into who He created us to be. He is the potter; we are the clay. He is the creator and has the **right** to mold us into whatever He desires.

Jer 18:4 (ESV) And the vessel he was making of clay was spoiled in the potter's hand, and he reworked it into another vessel, as it seemed good to the potter to do.

A gospel of self focuses on doing what makes you feel good, putting your needs and desires above others. It's "me" centered and "me" driven. In the true gospel of Jesus Christ, it is our desire to reproduce the character of Jesus. We must come to that place where we care about pleasing Him and building His Kingdom more than we care about our own fleshly desires.

We pour ourselves out so He can fill us with what He desires. There is a divine exchange that takes place as we surrender our self-life and take up the Christ-like life. When we surrender to

Him, He begins the process of forming us into who He wants us to be. It's a beautiful process as we grow into the full measure of the stature of Christ. We can be a vessel to be used by Him.

2Ti 2:21 (ESV) Therefore, if anyone cleanses himself from what is dishonorable, he will be a vessel for honorable use, set apart as holy, useful to the master of the house, ready for every good work.

It is God's desire that we become mature sons and daughters, strong in the Lord and no longer tossed to and fro by every wind of doctrine, the deceitfulness of men and craftiness of Satan. As you grow in God's completeness, the Holy Spirit assists in assigning you a training regiment uniquely designed and perfectly structured for your life assignment on earth. He also gives you the grace and faith to walk it out; one step at a time. It's the most fulfilling thing that you will ever do in life, not easy but well worth it!

Day 29
The Cross Cries Love

2 Corinthians 5:14 (TPT) For it is Christ's love that fuels our passion and motivates us, because we are absolutely convinced that he has given his life for all of us. 15 (NLT) He died for everyone so that those who receive his new life will no longer live for themselves. Instead, they will live for Christ, who died and was raised for them.

When you look at the cross do you see love? Do you see life or death? Jesus loved us so much that He gave His life for us. They didn't take His life, He freely gave it for me and for you. He took what we deserved (death) and gave us what He deserved (life).

It was His love for us that put Him on the cross. It was the perfect plan to restore what was lost so long ago in the first garden and He was willing and eager to do what needed to be done to earn back what was lost.

When I went to Israel, I stood in the Garden of Gethsemane and wept uncontrollably as I thought about how my Lord and Saviour walked that same ground and how He gave His life for me. Luke 22:44 (ESV) says *"his sweat became like great drops of blood falling down to the ground."* My life was forever changed as I stood beside those ancient olive trees with tears streaming down my face. I was marked for life and I determined right then and there to spend the rest of my life passionately living for Him.

Jesus wants your love. He wants you to have a passionate love for Him that cries out for Him. As I read the Psalms, I see the kind of love that David had for God. He had an intimate relationship and He lived to please God. He also craved God's presence.

So did Moses. Moses even said that if God would not go with him that he would not go. (Ex. 33:15) He knew that he needed God's help and the presence of God to go with him and before him or he would fail. How many times have we stepped out and gone without asking God to go with us only to realize later that we were not supposed to go there? God wants us tuned in to Him.

Psalms 51:16-17 (NLT) You do not desire a sacrifice, or I would offer one. You do not want a burnt offering. The sacrifice you desire is a broken spirit. You will not reject a broken and repentant heart, O God.

We need to learn to consult with God on all things. God spoke to Moses as man speaks to a friend. (Ex. 33:11) Do you consider God your friend? Do you have an intimate relationship with Him that allows you to really know Him and trust Him as someone that you can ask anything to? Is God real to you? Or is He just some fictitious character in a dusty book or someone you call upon only when angry or in distress?

You can start today by repenting and asking God to come into your heart in a real way. Then ask Him to baptize you with His gift of the Holy Spirit; a fresh baptism of fire, that's what you need! Then knock the dust off that sacred book, open that Bible up and start reading. That is His love letter to you. It contains the answers to all your questions.

Set your sights high and determine to yourself that you will fall in love with Jesus all over again. He's the one who gave His life for you; The one who died on that cross for you; The one who shed His blood and the Cross ran red for you. The cross cries out in love for you. You are His reward for dying on that cross. Will you now, in return, live your life for Him and become a man (or woman) after God's own heart ready to surrender yourself to Him and do all that He asks you to do? God is waiting for your response. Don't wait another day.

*Acts 13:22 (NLT) But God removed Saul and replaced him with David, a man about whom God said, 'I have found David son of Jesse, **a man after my own heart. He will do everything I want him to do.***

What does God say about you now? What does Heaven say? Ask God today to search your heart and make your motives pure before Him. Ask Him to set you on Fire for Him and help you to lay down your agenda and pick up His. God is looking for those who are obedient out of love and their only desire is to please their Father.

Ask God to forgive you for having such selfish motives and ambitions. Turn your heart to Him now and tell Him that you surrender your life to Him and you will do everything that He asks you to do from this moment forward. Then determine that you will do just that!

Day 30
Your Season of Job

Ecc 3:1 (KJV) To every thing there is a season, and a time to every purpose under the heaven:

God works in times and seasons, phases and stages in our lives for different purposes. He knows the perfect timing of things and every season has a purpose. Just as we have summer, spring, winter and fall, we have spiritual seasons too. The wilderness is a necessary season for maturity in the life of every believer. Every Child of God will be given seasons of wilderness. (Yes it's plural-more than one)

Job went through a very difficult season, as the Lord gave Satan permission to touch Job's possessions first and then his body. He destroyed all Job's livestock, servants and his children. Then he afflicted his body. This was not because Job was evil or had sinned. God actually presented him to Satan to test him. God knew Job well and He knew the position of Job's heart. He already knew how Job would respond.

Job 1:8 (ESV) And the LORD said to Satan, "Have you considered my servant Job, that there is none like him on the earth, a blameless and upright man, who fears God and turns away from evil?"

The animals that he owned represented his money, wealth and inheritance. As difficult as it was, Job didn't curse God, but he accepted his fate and cried out, "God gives and God takes away."

Job 1:22 (ESV) In all this Job did not sin or charge God with wrong.

My favorite scripture in *Job is 13:15 (KJV) Though he slay me, yet will I trust in him:*

Job may not have had a full understanding of why these things were happening but he trusted God. We can argue that it was because of pride, but the real reason is because God gave him over to Satan for a short season of testing. Not because he had sinned, as the Lord described Job as faithful. *"There is none like him on the earth, a blameless and upright man, who fears God and turns away from evil?" (Job 1:1 ESV)*

The fact is, God allowed him to go through this and after Job endured the process, God redeemed him, restored him and gave him a double blessing.

Job 42:10 (ESV) And the LORD restored the fortunes of Job, when he had prayed for his friends. And the LORD gave Job twice as much as he had before.

Look at the life of Apostle Paul. He was in a continuous stage of affliction. A messenger of Satan was assigned to him to harass or buffet him. (2 Cor. 7) His life journey, after his conversion, consisted of much affliction. His list was rather long and included being put in prison numerous times, being whipped many times without number, and he faced death again and again. Five different times the Jewish leaders gave him thirty-nine lashes. Three times he was beaten with rods. Once he was stoned. Three times he was shipwrecked. Once he spent a whole night and a day adrift at sea. He spent many sleepless nights cold and hungry. (2Cor. 11)

Satan wanted Peter too….Look what Jesus said about him. *Luke 22:31 (ESV) And the Lord said, Simon, Simon, behold, Satan hath desired (NASB says-demanded) to have you, that he may sift you like wheat:*

The trials you have been through were not designed to kill you and God didn't bring you this far to let the devil kill you. God is not punishing you or abandoning you. He hasn't forgotten you or disowned you. What you've been through has been hard, yet still, it's nothing compared to what Job or the Apostle Paul went through, or what Christ went through.

As you go through these trials, learn to stay focused on God and how to discern the times and the seasons, then you will know what He wants to accomplish in your life at that very moment. Learn it quickly so you don't lengthen your time in the wilderness.

Endure the process, change your perspective and believe that God will use it to move you forward and develop in you a solid foundation built on maturity, trust and humility, as you surrender it all to Him.

Complaining will only prolong your time in the wilderness. **Complaining is Satan's bread.** He feeds off of it and it brings in bitterness, doubt and unbelief.

*1Pe 5:10 (ESV) **After you have suffered for a little while,** the God of all grace, who called you to His eternal glory in Christ, will Himself perfect, confirm, strengthen and establish you.*

"After" you have suffered. First the process, then the promise. Allow God to strengthen you. He's trying to build something in you that is strong and stable, like a mighty fortress. Only God can do it. Could Job, on his own, give himself a double portion in return for his troubles? Could Paul get himself out of prison? Could Peter preach on his own authority and have thousands saved and healed and delivered? No, and neither can you.

Heb 10:36 (ESV) For you have need of endurance, so that when you have done the will of God you may receive what is promised.

Satan may have attacked you in every way, but God has the last laugh. He has the final say. Your portion is to endure and to stand and to believe. God does everything else. He is our king and His eye is on you and it's not over until God says it's over!
Stand strong mighty warrior! God will take everything that you have been through and use it for His Glory! Nothing wasted.

Day 31
Are You Kicking Against the Goads?

Act 26:14 (AMP) And when we had all fallen to the ground, I heard a voice in the Hebrew tongue saying to me, Saul, Saul, why do you continue to persecute Me [to harass and trouble and molest Me]? It is dangerous and turns out badly for you to keep kicking against the goads [to keep offering vain and perilous resistance].

A goad is not a term we use regularly. It is a farming implement used to spur or guide livestock. It is a long pointed stick or rod used to keep or turn animals in the proper direction and keep them on the path you want them on. Today we would call it a cattle prod.

Saul found himself in that predicament. He was persecuting God's people and fighting against God. He was empowered with governmental authority by the High Priest to persecute and arrest the followers of Christ and bring them to trial and he was determined to do just that.

Acts 9:1 (KJV) says, "And Saul, yet breathing out threatenings and slaughter against the disciples of the Lord...." He was on a rampage to stop or destroy those that he perceived to be misguided, yet all along, he was the one who was deceived and way off course.

He was doing what he thought was right and just. But he was totally deceived and out of the will of God when the light of Christ appeared and knocked him down and blinded him. God stepped in and stopped the abuse and persecution. Saul had an immediate career change. When people talk about their "Road to Damascus" experience, this is what they are referring to. It is the time when God, in an act of mercy, steps in and stops you from going your own way and abruptly changes your life course and turns you around. Have you ever been there?

When I think about the term "kicking against the goad", I think what it would be like to kick a sharp pointed object. Ouch! That would inflict pain and agony to your foot. It would be pointless (no pun intended) to kick a pointed object. In the natural, If you were to kick a sharp pointed object, you would inflict pain upon yourself and you would find yourself in a mess with a major foot injury. That is what we do when we go our own way and ignore God and His divine calling for our lives. Why do we keep doing something knowing that it brings pain and hurt to ourselves and others?

If you have found yourself running from God or not wanting to accept your destiny and just wanting to go your own way and do your own thing, you have probably found yourself kicking against the goad. How has that turned out for you? Probably not too good.

It is God's desire for you to stop doing what is against His will and causing you pain and grief; then repent and make a divine turnaround. Turn back to God and allow Him to lead you to where He wants you to go. Surrender yourself fully to Him and His ways and watch your life turnaround for the better.

Remember, goads or prods are used for rebellious and stubborn animals that refuse to follow their good shepherd. Don't find yourself there, turn before it's too late. God is waiting on you to run into His arms! Like a good Father, He will always receive you back and put you on His path to your destiny.

Day 32
Giants Will Fall

Before you can cross over or transition into your Promised Land, there are some Giants that have to be taken down. Are you ready to face your giants? Are you ready to take down those giants that have held you captive and buffeted you? I'm here to tell you that the devil is after your inheritance. He is out to destroy you and everything that you love and have worked for.

The question is, Are you going to allow him to get away with it? Satan is a bully and he works off of intimidation and fear. We must stand up to evil or it will overcome us.

There are many enemies that you will face on the road to your inheritance and destiny. Many giants will challenge you and have to be taken out along the way. You must become a "Giant Slayer." Like Joshua, you too will be faced with many evil "ite"-nations that have to be dealt with along the way to your destiny.

This was part of God's instructions to the people of Israel before they could take the Promised Land. We all have giants to face, individually and corporately. We must be willing and able to confront and overtake these evil spirits that come to destroy us.

Deut. 7:1–2 (ESV) When The Lord your God brings you into the land that you are about to enter and occupy, and he clears away many nations before you—the Hittites, the Girgashites, the

*Amorites, the Canaanites, the Perizzites, the Hivites, and the Jebusites, seven nations mightier and more numerous than you... then you must **utterly destroy** them. Make no covenant with them and show them no mercy.*

When the Israelites came out of Egypt, they had a slave mentality. After over 400 years in Egypt, they had lost their warrior mentality. They had to learn how to trust God and rely on Him for everything. They also had to realize that they were not worthless slaves anymore but Sons of the Living God.

There are many things that will destroy you and your call and cause you to abort your God given assignment. You cannot turn the other cheek or ignore giants that are determined to kill you. Passivity never wins a "Giant" war. Just as the Lord told Joshua, to show them no mercy, you too must overcome them.

When God tells you to "utterly destroy" something (that is serious) and If you don't, then you put yourself under the power of it and it will utterly destroy you. It's serious to disobey God. Partial obedience is still disobedience.

When we become Christians, we enlist into God's army. We are born again onto the battlefield. The choice is not whether we want to enter into a conflict or not, the war has already been declared against us. Our only choice is whether we want to be trampled by the enemy or learn how to fight and win.

Warfare is real and it will take you out if you allow it. There is the internal battle that we have with our old mind, thoughts and habits; our fleshly weaknesses, then there are the external battles we fight where the enemy comes to destroy us. Both are real.

When you accepted God as your Savior, the battle intensified. Becoming a Christian and confessing your faith will attract demons sent to distract you, discourage you and even take you out if possible. It is serious. But God always has a plan to get you to where He has desired you to be. Warfare will strengthen you and mature you into that mighty warrior that God has created you to be.

We have to get rid of the "ites" to be able to follow God fully. There can be no division, no competition, no offense, no jealousy, no unforgiveness, no bitterness. All of these will stop the flow of the Holy Spirit and render us useless on the battlefield. It's a process and God knows exactly how to heal you and set you free.

Ex. 23:30 (NIV) Little by little I will drive them out before you, until you have increased enough to take possession of the land.

It Starts with YOU. You must be the one who gets rid of the "ites" that you are carrying within yourself. Don't focus on others, focus on yourself. You must be the one who casts down the spirits of Jezebel, fear, insecurity, false identity, sabotage, anger, pride, competition, jealousy, false humility, rejection, apathy, complacency, and political and religious spirits inside YOU.

YOU must be the one to get healed and then from there it will go outward to your family, your church, your region, then to the nation. You want to get Jezebel out of your region? Get the Jezebel out of YOU.

We must walk in a spirit of discernment. We must be wise to the schemes, the plots and the tactics of the enemy. It is critical for your walk so you don't become a needless casualty of war.

Let today be the day that you begin your new journey to your Promised Land; Your God-given place of destiny. Let God come inside you in a real way and begin to change you from the inside out. It always starts with ourselves. Ask God, "What is inside of me that is not of you Lord?' Then ask him to take it and begin the transformation process of turning you into the person that He created you to be! You will not regret it!

His Reflection

As I face the mirror on the wall,
Help me Lord to fulfill the Call.
Show me what's inside of me.
Examine my heart so I will see
The Truth...

Give me the strength to look within
So the process may begin.
As I surrender it all to thee,
Seal me, mark me, make me be
Like You...

Our hearts connect and beat as one,
Thanks to the Gift from The Son.
Until in the glass It's no longer me,
But a reflection of you I see.
I'm yours.....

Day 33
Anger is a Destroyer

James 1:19 (ESV) Know this, my beloved brothers: let every person be quick to hear, slow to speak, slow to anger;

Anger is a negative emotion often characterized by feelings of great displeasure, indignation, hostility, fear, and vengeance. Many times, reacting in anger is how we express our dissatisfaction with life. It's defined in the Greek language as the strongest of all passions. Anger begins with a feeling that escalates into a reaction.

Ecc 7:9 (ESV) Be not quick in your spirit to become angry, for anger lodges in the heart of fools.

When we think of anger, mostly we think of rage or an outburst or losing our temper which is usually how it manifests. But it can also manifest in other ways such as clamming up, getting depressed, or using the silent treatment. Holding things in is also very destructive. It will cause you to want to explode and even cause sickness and disease in your body.

Keeping anger locked inside and pretending it doesn't exist can be dangerous to our health also. Most of the time, we're only hurting ourselves, and the person who angered us isn't even aware of our pain. So we must take responsibility for our anger and learn to deal with it properly. We must give it to God and allow Him to deal with it and bring that forgiveness and closure that will relieve the pressure and bring the healing.

All through the Bible there are examples of anger destroying lives. It opens the doors to other sins and will overtake people and cause them to lose their destiny. Anger, when harbored, leads to death and destruction.

Cain was jealous and angry with Abel. He killed him and then lied about it. God warned him and gave him a chance to redeem himself. He encouraged him to rule over his fleshly desires, but he chose not to. We have the same choice today.

Gen 4:7 (ESV) If you do well, will you not be accepted? And if you do not do well, sin is crouching at the door. Its desire is for you, but you must rule over it."

Naaman almost lost his healing because he became angry and offended. He didn't like the way the Prophet Elisha brought his healing. He thought he was important enough for the man of God to come personally to him. (He took on offense)

*2Ki 5:10 (ESV) And Elisha sent a messenger to him, saying, "Go and wash in the Jordan seven times, and your flesh shall be restored, and you shall be clean." 11 But Naaman **was angry** and went away, saying, "Behold, I thought that he would surely come out to me and stand and call upon the name of the LORD his God, and wave his hand over the place and cure the leper.*

Don't lose your healing because you don't like the way God does it. Don't lose your blessing because you don't like the way God delivers it. Don't lose your miracle because you don't like the way God packages it. Miracles come in strange packages sometimes! God will test your mind and your heart, checking your level of humility and obedience. He will check the motives of your heart and search for anything that is not of Him.

Moses' anger caused him to lose his entrance into the Promised Land (Numbers 20:8-12) He was disobedient and struck the rock, when God said to speak to it. Anger and frustration caused him to be disobedient to the Lord which was a costly mistake. Don't let the enemy steal your destiny, by walking in anger.

Realize that you can have control by walking in the Spirit and not returning evil for evil but living peaceably with all. (Rom 12:17-21) When you begin to feel anger rising up, it's the perfect time to exercise the fruit of the Spirit and self-control.(Gal 5:22-24) You may even have a good reason to be angry, but don't use it as an excuse to stay that way. Don't deny it or justify it, just ask God to help you deal with it and cast it down.

Don't harbor anger, jealousy, resentment, hatred, bitterness, unforgiveness, or any other negative emotion that separates you from God. They will hold you back from fulfilling your destiny, steal your blessings and keep you from moving forward in the things of God. Give it all to God and allow Him to take it and turn it around and use it for His Glory.

Day 34
Destination Glory

Luk 4:18 (KJV) The Spirit of the Lord is upon me, because he hath anointed me to preach the gospel to the poor; he hath sent me to heal the brokenhearted, to preach deliverance to the captives, and recovering of sight to the blind, to set at liberty them that are bruised, 19 To preach the acceptable year of the Lord.

Jesus came to heal the broken-hearted and set the captives free. No matter what you've been through in life, God will take your tragedy and turn it into triumph. He will take Your mess and turn it into a message, your test into a testimony. He's a transforming God and that's what He does best- transform lives!

When you turn your life over to Jesus, your testimony will give other people hope for their desperate situation and you can help other people find healing and victory through your hurts and wounds. Jesus said that we would do greater things than what He did. I often wondered what it was that we could do that would be greater than the works of Jesus? Then I thought of how He didn't have a testimony. He could not say: Once I was lost but now I'm found; I was addicted and God delivered me; or I was blind but now I see. We can take everything in our lives and point them back to Jesus and what He did for us.

Your greatest life messages will come out of your deepest hurts and pain. Satan meant to destroy you, but Jesus will use it to empower you!

Rev 12:11 (KJV) And they overcame him by the blood of the Lamb, and by the word of their testimony; and they loved not their lives unto the death.

There is a way to get back at Satan for all the pain and hurt that he has caused you: Surrender your life to God and become the devil's worst nightmare! Tell as many people as you can about Jesus and what He has done for you.

Let that very thing the devil meant to destroy you, make you stronger. Let that very thing the enemy thought would kill you, bring you life. Let that very thing Satan sent to silence you, only made you bolder and louder for God!

What Satan didn't count on was you turning to God and letting Him heal your hurts and your pains. He wanted you to get bitter at God and he wanted to ruin your life and steal your destiny.

Even though Satan may take some ground and win some battles-God wins the war! We've read the back of the book and God wins!

Satan may bruise your heel, but you can stomp on his head by the power of The Cross. I believe every church needs some devil stompers! Jesus came to set us free and to bring healing and wholeness and to destroy the works of the devil.

1John 3:8b (ESV) The reason the Son of God appeared was to destroy the works of the devil.

Why not determine today, right now that you will surrender yourself to God as a living sacrifice, holy and acceptable unto God? (Rom 12:1) You are either on God's side or Satan's side. There is no middle ground. To not take a side or to try and remain neutral puts you in the devil's playground and opens doors for him to attack you.

However, you have a choice. Determine that you will live your life for God in such a radical way that you become the devil's worst nightmare.

God has given us numerous tools for defeating the enemy. First of all, we are to take up the whole armor of God and learn to use His Word like a sword.(Eph 6) Praise and Worship are powerful weapons to defeat the enemy. Powerful prophetic Prayers and decrees will shift the atmosphere and reroute the enemy and his tactics too.

What is your choice? As for me, I'm determined to continue my fight against Satan and his kingdom of darkness and help as many people as possible get saved, set free and delivered and set on fire for God. My destination is Glory and this process will continue until I get there! What is your destination?

Day 35
Who Will Rule Your Region?

Today you must decide who will rule your region. It's a Mount Carmel moment. The Lord is saying, *"How long will you go limping between two different opinions? If the LORD is God, follow him; but if Baal, then follow him." (1 Kings 18:21)*

You may be thinking, What can I do? How can I make a difference? I am here to tell you today that you can make a difference. Go look in the mirror and say "It's going to start with me. As for me and my house, we will serve the Lord and I decree that Jesus Christ is King of my house and my region." It starts with one. We each have a circle of influence. It could be very small or very large, the size doesn't matter. It's your circle and you must determine that God will rule in your circle and if we each do that, my circle will intersect your circle and your circle will intersect someone else's circle and they will begin to overlap and come together and blanket our nation and we will become "One Nation Under God," again.

God is looking for some people, some radical people that are not scared to storm the gates of hell; Those who can believe with Him and have radical faith. Those who will tear down those false altars in their cities. They will stand firm against the enemy and his tactics and say "NO you don't Satan. Not in my city."

God is calling those Believers who will shift the climate of their regions. They are the ones who will pray and fast and walk the streets of their cities and declare that no evil will come near there. They will boldly declare their city will be drug free, crime free and a cancer free zone and the healthiest city in their state.

When the great healing evangelist, John G. Lakes, came on the scene in Spokane WA, in 1915, and started the Healing Rooms, he shifted that city. It became known as the healthiest city in America because of the prayers and the faith and the bold authority that the Saints of God walked in. We can do that again. God wants us to.

We must change our thinking, God is not small and with God backing you, neither are you. Gideon didn't think he could do anything either. He thought very lowly of himself. He had been beat down and was full of fear and insecurity. Where he saw a useless coward, God saw a warrior. Where he saw hopelessness, God saw hope. ***What Some call misfits, God calls mighty.*** **God works wonders with weak, broken, forgotten vessels.**

Jdg 6:14 (ESV) And the LORD turned to him and said, "Go in this might of yours and save Israel from the hand of Midian; do not I send you? 15 And he said to him, "Please, Lord, how can I save Israel? Behold, my clan is the weakest in Manasseh, and I am the least in my father's house."

We get all messed up and off track when we start comparing ourselves with others. We see ourselves as small and unimportant, even worthless at times. We become the grasshoppers and they become the giants. That's why it's so important to keep our focus on God and what He has called us to do. It's not what you see or how you feel, it's what He says that counts.

When the spies were sent out to the Promised Land, they had to choose between the giants and the fruit. Would they focus on the evil or the good? That's what it all comes down to. We have to choose, do we want to focus on the goodness of God or the evil of this world?

Joshua and Caleb said, " The land flows with milk and honey, the fruit is huge. There are some giants there, but so what, God says it's ours. Let us go up at once and occupy it, for we are well able to overcome it." The other 10 said, "We can't do this, they are stronger and bigger than us. The land devours its inhabitants, and all the people that we saw in it are like giants and we seemed to ourselves like grasshoppers, and so we seemed to them." (Num 13)

It was their _perception_ of how the giants saw them that caused them to destroy and delay the destiny of a whole nation. We must stick with what God says, even when it looks like, in the natural, there is no way it can happen. Remember what God's Word says:

Luke 1:37 (AMP) For with God nothing is ever impossible and no word from God shall be without power or impossible of fulfillment.

Today, surrender yourself to God again. Repent for your unbelief and doubt. Rise up and say I can make a difference and I will make a difference. Thank you Father for filling me with strength for this journey. I can do this. My region will be more like Heaven because

I stand up and declare that Jesus Christ is King here and across this nation.

Day 36
David's Greatest Accomplishment

David's greatest accomplishment was not bringing down Goliath or conquering the enemies of God, It was when he brought God's heavenly throne, the Ark of the Covenant, to The City of David in Jerusalem.

The first time David attempted to transport the Ark back to Jerusalem, he made a costly mistake. He did not seek God on how to properly carry the Ark of God's presence. He learned that lesson the hard way, as one of the men, while at the threshing floor, reached out to steady the Ark. It was as though a lightning bolt from Heaven struck him and split him in two. God's presence, the Ark, was not to be handled carelessly then, **nor is it now**.

David was so distraught over the death of Uzzah that he fearfully abandoned the Ark at Obed-edom's house. He was blessed abundantly while it was there for 3 months.
(1 Chr 13:14) Your house will be blessed too if you choose to allow God's presence to reside there. You must invite the King of Glory to come in and dwell among you in your homes and businesses. He's waiting for His invitation now. Go ahead.

David was afraid and angry but when he realized his mistake in carrying the Ark. He sought The Lord and God was faithful to show him the proper way to carry His presence. David was determined to get the Ark home, where it belonged. But he knew it had to be done precisely as God instructed.

There will be times, when you are carrying the presence of God, that you will be deceived, make wrong decisions and even costly mistakes. There are some things that can only be learned by experience, you can't read it in a book or even just have someone explain it or teach it to you. You have to "live it," as you walk through it on your own.

Even today, God's presence is holy and pure and must be handled with care. ***How well you carry the fiery presence of The Holy God will be your greatest challenge and accomplishment.*** You too must hear God's voice and obey, for You are a glory carrier. That same Spirit that raised Jesus from the dead lives inside you! (Rom 8:11) That's so powerful!

As a matter of fact, in your belly, is the perfect DNA gift mix that God Himself designed specifically for you. God has already created in you the perfect DNA mixture to reach the people that He has assigned to you. He is sending them to you. Get ready. You are like the perfect drink offering, the perfect alabaster box and the perfect vessel, all made by the master's hands.

We probably carry some of the same Revival DNA too. It seems as though God links people by assignments, tribes and sounds and callings. Since you have made it this far along in this journey, chances are that we may be a DNA match. That means that we are drawn to the same things of God, attracted to the same sounds and carry the same Fire of God and have similar assignments. Just as those mighty men made their way to the cave of Adullam, seeking healing, freedom and purpose, you have made your way to this page, seeking answers and looking for some things that have been missing in your life. I pray that God gives you the answers you need to walk out your calling and complete your assignment.

I may carry something deep within me that you need and you may carry something just as valuable that I need to fulfill my purpose. With God there is always a reciprocal exchange in the spirit when a true relationship is formed. It's never all one sided, where you give and I take. That's not Kingdom, that worldly— and slavery.

God has a way of connecting people according to their assignments. I thank God for those He connected me with along my journey. He brought in those to teach, train and equip me and to hold up my arms when I grew weary; Intercessors who could pray the house down; Worshippers who's sound could pierce the darkness and tear down strongholds; Apostles and prophets and teachers to train, equip and strengthen me and yes even correct me along the way. (They are still doing that:)

The beauty of the kingdom of God is that God gives you an assignment and as you step out in faith and do it, you will grow and mature. Then He gives you another and another and one step at a time, He builds you up and leads you to your purpose. Everything you do for the Kingdom of God is significant. There are no insignificant assignments in God's Kingdom. If God has put His finger on it, then it's significant.

David may have messed up trying to carry God's presence in his own way but God revealed to him the better way and David made a course correction. He tried again and every step led him one step closer to his destination. Along the path to your destiny, there will be numerous opportunities to quit and give up. David learned that he must take a few steps, stop and offer a sacrifice of thanksgiving to God for every small accomplishment. (2Sam 6:13) We must learn this too and we must learn how to persevere through the storms.

I find it interesting that it was at the threshing floor that Uzzah touched the Ark and was killed. (2Sam 6:6) It's during those times of testings and struggles that we must keep our focus on God and our destiny and not get distracted and careless in our decisions.

I Thank God that David didn't give up after his first attempted failure. He was determined to complete his assignment and get the Ark of God's presence to its proper place as ordained by God. David's greatest life accomplishment was bringing the Ark to The City of David in Jerusalem. It set the course for the rest of his life.

David was serious about his assignment and I pray that you are too. He organized 4000 musicians and 288 singers to minister to God in David's tent 24/7 in shifts or watches. They were full time intercessory worshippers and David supported them all.

The key of David was 24/7 worship before the presence of the Lord in the tabernacle of David. It was passionate and unbridled worship that unlocked the power of the heavenly realm and released God's presence for the people of God. David discovered that worship was the key.

David unlocked the heavenly realm using praise, worship, intercession and proclamations from God's Word. Thereby accessing what was already in heaven and by faith, establishing that heavenly realm here on this earth, bringing it into manifestation on the earth.

1Ch 16:8 (ESV) Oh give thanks to the LORD; call upon his name; make known his deeds among the peoples! 9 Sing to him, sing praises to him; tell of all his wondrous works! 10 Glory in his holy name; let the hearts of those who seek the LORD rejoice.

God is looking for those who are passionately and intimately in love with Him to return that Worship Revolution back to the earth. It is a revelatory breakthrough of man to access the heavenly realm.

The sound of the prophetic, spirit filled worship, are the frequencies that resonate with heaven. The decreeing of the Word of God in the tabernacle of David, literally **shook and dismantled evil strongholds and pierced through to the glory realm and you can do the same thing.** I too have heard sounds that shook every fiber of my being as they permeated the atmosphere and toppled faulty foundations and strongholds. There's a sound that comes directly from the Throne of God and when it intersects with God's perfect timing, there's an explosion in the spirit realm. I love it when we find that and experience that. That's what the true prophetic does.

David's Tabernacle became an open portal from Heaven. Heaven manifested itself and became reality on the earth through the tent of David. God's presence filled that tent. The Ark was the place where heaven touched earth. It's referred to as His Throne and also His footstool.

If David could establish the Throne of God in the Old Testament, then it can also be established today in our cities. Lift up your voices to Him in praise and thanksgiving. It's not about a perfect performance. It's about a perfectly surrendered heart; One positioned in the hands of God that is humbly seeking and eagerly anticipating the manifestation of God's Glory.

Psa 22:3 (KJV) But thou art holy, O thou that inhabitest the praises of Israel.

God is looking for those laid down lovers who crave being in His presence and who are crying out for His Glory. The time has come to put God back in His proper place in this nation and in the earth.

John 4:23 (ESV) But the hour is coming, and is now here, when the true worshipers will worship the Father in spirit and truth, for the Father is seeking such people to worship him.

Worship is important to the Lord. It reveals the position of your heart and It releases His glory! The hour is now and you my friend are here for such a time as this.

Rise up mighty warrior. **It is not time to be silent, It's time to roar!**

Day 37
Are You A Spear Thrower or a Spear Dodger?

Psalms 139:23-24 (AMP) Search me [thoroughly], O God, and know my heart; Test me and know my anxious thoughts; And see if there is any wicked or hurtful way in me, And lead me in the everlasting way.

David's heart was being tested over and over again just as your heart is being tested now. Would he touch Gods anointed? Would he strike back at King Saul? Would he pick up the spear that was meant to nail him to the wall and throw it back at this mad king? After all, David had been anointed King too.

Everybody knows what to do when someone throws a spear at you. Everyone has been taught by peers, media and society how to handle that, right? The world knows that you pick it up and throw it back. However, David did not, because His heart was in the right position with God and we shouldn't either. We aren't supposed to live like the world does, we are citizens of another kingdom, one that operates with love and honor.

Satan has people looking at each other, judging each other, being critical of other people, ministers and ministries while God is looking for those who will show love and honor and respect to all regardless of the circumstances.

Luke 6:45 (NLT) A good person produces good things from the treasury of a good heart, and an evil person produces evil things from the treasury of an evil heart. What you say flows from what is in your heart.

David never sat around with his people and criticized King Saul. Even though he knew in his heart what Saul was doing wasn't right. **Yet he valued God's judgement more than his own**. He knew that God removes kings and God sets up kings. (Dan 2:21) David knew in his heart that it was not his place to take Saul out.

We judge others and criticize them just because we don't like the way they do ministry or we think it should be done differently or we don't like the music or the carpet or the chairs or their gender or their color or the way they talk. (Any excuse will do for some people)

But the truth is, you don't really know the end from the beginning. You don't really know whether God is with them or not. I'm not talking about open blatant sin here. I'm talking about judging other people's hearts. Someone crosses our path and in all of our self-righteousness and self exaltation, we think that God put them there for us to straighten them out or help them, when in reality, God may have put them there to test YOUR heart. You never fully know who the test is for and God never tells. So you have to learn to walk it out so that either way you pass God's test.

Jeremiah 17:9-10 (NLT) The human heart is the most deceitful of all things, and desperately wicked. Who really knows how bad it is? But I, the Lord, search all hearts and examine secret motives. I give all people their due rewards, according to what their actions deserve.

Of course we can know them by their fruits- be a fruit inspector- as some people like to say. But see, **every person you meet is fighting a battle that you know nothing about**. Your words can bring life or death; blessings or cursings; Encouragement or discouragement. In the natural, words hurt nearly as much as spears. They can tear down or build up. They can pin you to a wall that you never get free from.

Some people want to judge or criticize or correct and that's not always their place. We need to learn to love people through the process. God accepted you that way. The process is not always pretty. People make mistakes. They say and do dumb things. Immaturity and rebellion sometimes manifest similar characteristics. Wisdom will show you which one you are dealing with. Immature people will humble themselves. Rebellious people will not.

It's Jesus's desire to take us from where we are to where He wants us to be. God is looking for those who are sold out to him, like David was. Those who will come humbly before Him; Not haughty and thinking that they have it all figured out, when in reality they have very little knowledge, compared to God.

We may walk by a homeless person or rough looking character and cast judgement upon them and cast them out into outer darkness. While God can take a drug dealer with a needle still in his arm, and touch him and raise him up to save a generation.

Let's learn to lift each other up and help each other. We all need to walk with a spirit of love and honor among all people.

John 13:35 (ESV) By this all people will know that you are my disciples, if you have love for one another.

As a leader, we must learn to listen to what people say AND watch what they do. What's inside will come out when a little pressure is applied. What's in their heart (and yours) will be exposed. This goes for everyone. Your portion is to obey God, love others, help those in need as directed by God, be the best YOU that you can be— with God's help and Don't throw spears or fire ugly words at others. Instead, give God your heart, guard your tongue and stay in your lane by only doing what God tells you to do.

Mat 12:34 You snakes! You are so evil. How can you say anything good? What people say with their mouths comes from what fills their hearts.

Dodging spears can cause offense and bitterness to set in. Once you harbor that ugly spirit and take hold of it, then Anger jumps in the game along with his brothers Rage and Murder. Next thing you know, you too have become a spear thrower. God tested David's heart continuously until He was confident that David would not become a spear thrower like Saul. God will test your heart too. I hope and pray that you pass His test.

Day 38
The Freedom is in the Forgiving

Mar 11:25 (ESV) And whenever you stand praying, forgive, if you have anything against anyone, so that your Father also who is in heaven may forgive you your trespasses."

Unforgiveness is a bitter root. It's a poison that will ruin your health and steal your joy and cause a bitterness to settle deep in your soul.

Forgiveness if not for the other person, it's for you. In releasing them, you have released yourself. **We must forgive because Christ forgave us.**

When you don't forgive them, God can't forgive you. Your job is to release them, get before God and get your heart right, then keep moving forward. Your freedom does not depend on their resolution- it depends on your resolution with God. It doesn't matter whether they receive it or not, once you release them, then it's between them and God.

Matthew 6:14-15 (NLT) If you forgive those who sin against you, your heavenly Father will forgive you. But if you refuse to forgive others, your Father will not forgive your sins.

When you forgive someone, you are not letting them off the hook, but giving them over to God. It's as though you carry them and lay them at the feet of Jesus. Now you are released from them and they are in the hands of God.

To forgive, doesn't mean you have to condone their sin. It doesn't mean they were right and you were wrong. It just means that you choose not to harbor that any longer; you choose to let it go and let God deal with it.

When you forgive, you are helping yourself, but you are also releasing that other person so that God can do what He does best in bringing healing and wholeness to their lives. If you're in the way by trying to get revenge or taking care of the situation yourself instead of trusting and obeying God, then He has no obligation to deal with that person. Because we know that vengeance doesn't belong to us, it belongs to the Lord. *(Rom 12:19)*

However, God will deal with those who hurt us, if we put them in His hands through forgiveness. The act of forgiving is our **seed** of obedience to His Word. Once we've **sown our seed**, He is faithful to bring a harvest of blessing to us **His Way.** You reap what you sow, good or bad... sow mercy, you get mercy... sow judgement, you get judgement.

Forgiveness also helps me by allowing God to do His work in me. Unforgiveness, if harbored, will cause a spiritual roadblock in your life. It's a poison and will cause bitterness to set in and even resentment, retaliation, anger, hatred, violence and murder if harbored long enough. Not to mention the physical aspect of it. Bitterness is a key root to disease.

Your fellowship with God can be hindered or blocked by Unforgiveness. You don't want that. It's not worth it.

In order to be healed, You must make a conscientious decision to forgive and let go. It's a choice. Not because they deserve it or you feel like it. But because that's what God wants you to do and it's necessary in order for you to fulfill your destiny. Just make a quality decision to forgive and allow God to heal your wounded heart. Go to God and say, I forgive them or Help me to forgive them Lord." Just because you forgive them, it doesn't mean they were right and you were wrong. That has nothing to do with forgiving.

John 20:22-23 (NLT) Then he breathed on them and said, "Receive the Holy Spirit. If you forgive anyone's sins, they are forgiven. If you do not forgive them, they are not forgiven.

Ask God to breathe upon you and allow the Holy Spirit to infill you and heal you so you can be made whole. Then Pray for those who hurt you. Pray for their healing and happiness and well being, Not that God would bring them down. It's not God's desire that any be lost.

Luke 6:27 (ESV) But I say to you who hear, Love your enemies, do good to those who hate you, 28 bless those who curse you, pray for those who abuse you.

As you pray a sincere heartfelt prayer and forgiveness comes, God can give those who came against you revelation that will bring them out of deception. They may not even be aware that they hurt you, or maybe they are so self-centered that they don't care.

BUT either way, God can give them revelation. They too can be healed and set free.

It's CRITICAL that you do not speak cursings against them or anyone else, but speak only blessings. Just so there's NO misunderstands, Blessings means "to speak well of "and "cursings means to speak evil of." You can't walk in true forgiveness and be a gossip. Learn to let things go. **Every person is walking a walk that you know nothing about.**

The words that come out of our mouth reveal what's in our hearts. Speaking evil or being critical of someone is not praying for them. Gossiping is not praying for them. If we harbor Unforgiveness then evil will come out. We will be held accountable for our words, they will be classified as Blessings or Cursings....

Mat 12:36 (ESV) I tell you, on the day of judgment people will give account for every careless word they speak, 37 for by your words you will be justified, and by your words you will be condemned.

Forgive God if you are angry with Him that your life hasn't turned out like you expected it to or thought it should. You may even have to forgive an object or a situation, such as a store that cheated you, a car that broke down on you and caused you trouble, the post office for losing your package etc. Ask Holy Spirit to show you. Go ahead and do that now. I'll wait.

Empty yourself out of all the poison that comes from bitterness, resentment, and Unforgiveness. Guard your heart and protect it, from the spiritual bitterness of Unforgiveness. Get washed in the water, the river of God, the water of His Word and His love and forgiveness and stay clean and close to God.

Heb 12:15 See to it that no one fails to obtain the grace of God; that no "root of bitterness" springs up and causes trouble, and by it many become defiled;

God is here now waiting on you to forgive that other person. Go ahead and do that now. You can't afford to wait another day. You have an assignment waiting for you.

Day 39
What I have Learned

Sometimes when we hear God or get a prophetic word, we don't really have a complete understanding of what He is trying to tell us. It takes time to unpack it and see the full manifestation of it. Due to our life experiences and woundedness, we see through the glass dimly. But as we hold that word in our hearts and ponder it and let it marinate and expand and allow God to fully develop it into our inner man, over time we will see God's true intent for it. Some prophetic words are like seeds and they take years to mature to fruit.

Years ago while walking the beach, I heard the Lord say, "I saved you alone, I called you alone and now you need to learn to be alone with me. " I pondered that in my heart and thought I had an understanding of it. Then God took me on a wilderness "adventure" for several years and I discovered I knew very little at all. Yet I continued to seek God's full revelation on it.

Recently as I walked that same beach, God reminded me of that word He had given me years earlier. Holy Spirit began unpacking that to me at a much greater and deeper level and My faith was challenged as I began to seek His complete meaning and purpose for my life.

If we are really fortunate and blessed in life, we have a spouse or kids or a few close friends or mentors that we can have those deep, intimate conversations with and truly share our hearts with. Cherish that, It is a rare precious jewel- a gift from God.

But for the most part, most people live a secret life that is hidden deep within and never gets tapped to be released to its fullest potential, which is what God desires.
There's a well inside you that wants to spring up and out!

I know this doesn't apply to all of us, but at one time or another most of us can relate to some of this. (Thank God for inner healing) There have been times we put on a smile and a happy face when we are around others yet on the inside we are a big mess. We have kids who are hurting, struggling, in abusive relationships or won't even talk to us or think we are insane. We despise our jobs and our finances are in a mess, we have addictions or hidden sins that we brush off or refuse to face and admit. We are constantly fighting with thoughts of depression or even suicide while walking in pride, rebellion and unforgiveness.

The struggles are real. Life is hard. We get hurt and it takes a minute or two (or a lifetime) to get back up sometimes and if the truth be known, some things we never fully get over or recover from.

Yet, through it all, I've learned a few things;

I've learned to love people, even when they are down right mean. I've learned to always keep my heart tender to the things of God. I've learned that it's OK to love people who don't love you back. I've learned that we overcome evil with good. I've learned that I don't know everything and I'm not always right and I can't fix people, only God can. It's not my portion to fix, it's my portion to love. Most importantly, I've learned not to just say I believe the Word and God, but to live it. Actions really do speak louder than words. My beliefs and my love for God are best shown in my daily walk.

Jas 4:17 So whoever knows the right thing to do and fails to do it, for him it is sin.

I've learned that God is real and He wants the best for me. I've learned to allow God to come into those hidden places and bring healing and wholeness to all areas of my life and to put my faith in the one who will never leave me or forsake me. I've learned that Holy Spirit is always with me and He is my best teacher, counselor, comforter and friend. He always listens and He always talks and He's never rude or controlling like some people can be. I've learned it's best to just stay away from some people, bless them and love them from a distance. I've learned that people will hurt you, even the ones that you love and have helped, but love them and help them anyway.

I've learned that God knows best and His ways are higher than my ways. I've learned to laugh more, to love more and even to cry more. (Tears are healing) I've learned that people will disappoint you, but God will not. I've learned that people are not my Holy Spirit and I cannot be their Holy Spirit either. I've learned that there is a place, a void, in each of us that only God can fill. Nothing else will do.

I've learned that God is a covenant keeping God who is searching for covenant keeping people. I've learned the real meaning of entering into a covenant with God. I've learned that it's Ok to hurt and I now understand a little more how Job felt when he said, "Though He slay me I will trust Him." (Job 13:15)

And when I look back on this journey a few years from now, then too will I realize that my understanding was shallow and limited because I will have moved to a deeper and more intimate place with the Father because that is where He is taking me and also where I desire to go; A place where I lay my head on His chest and be so close that I can hear and feel His heart beat for me; my family, my region and my nation.

Right now, Why not lift your hands and say, "Take me higher Lord! Take me deeper Lord! I want more of you! I surrender my life fully to you today and I enter into a covenant with you Lord to fulfill your plans for me and to become who you created me to be and to help others do the same!"

Ask God to take you there. Start talking and communing with the Holy Spirit as though He's your best friend. Form that relationship with the one that the Father sent you when Jesus returned to Heaven. Your life will never be the same and you will discover your purpose and God's plan for your life. You will be so glad you did! Get ready! It's a wonderful ride!

Day 40
Tell Them We're Coming and Heaven's Coming With us!

God is a warrior and warriors reproduce warriors! God is preparing His Bride for a war and a wedding simultaneously. It's not time to stand down or back down, it's time to take a stand. Just like the dry bones in the valley with Ezekiel, God has prophesied breath and spirit into you and you will rise up on your feet and become part of that great army of God. I say right now, "Dry bones come alive!"

Exo 15:3 The LORD is a man of war (a warrior): the LORD is his name.

Jesus is also coming back as a warrior!

*Rev 19:11 Then I saw heaven opened, and behold, a white horse! The one sitting on it is called Faithful and True, and in righteousness **he judges and makes war**.*

God is raising up an Army of Warriors, a new breed of passionate lovers of God who will rise up and boldly declare, " Jesus is King." We need strong, determined men and women of God, whose hearts are strong enough to face whatever firepower Satan throws at them.

One of the wonderful things about the Kingdom of God is that everyone has an assignment that is conducive to where they are at that very moment in their walk. As they step out in obedience and do what God calls them to do, it will grow as they grow, spiritually. Although God sometimes has to nudge us in the right direction or hold us back or even pick us up and put us back on the path at times, He always meets us where we are, then begins the process of taking us to where He wants us to be. Just remember, Your current location is not your final destination.

I thank God for the warfare and the wilderness seasons I have been through. They made me stronger and drew me closer to God. **After they were over**, I could say, " Thank you God. " But during the process, I felt the pain, then afterwards I saw the promise. There will always be pain associated with your promise. God is trying to build us up, mature us into mighty men and women of God. We might start off as babies, but God wants us to grow up, be strong in the Lord and not be tossed around by every wind of doctrine. God wants us strong, resolute and determined to finish our race. After all, The Finisher lives on the inside of each one of us!

God is raising up some David's and some Joshua's and some Caleb's and some Deborah's and some Esther's who fear God more than they fear the giants they have to face. They will run toward the enemies, not away from them. I thank God that there are those who are willing to do whatever it takes to see the kingdom of Heaven come to earth.

I love David's passion. When confronted by this God-mocking giant, He asks a simple question, " Is there not a cause?" (1 Sam 17:29) What are you so passionate about that you are willing to lay down your life for? There was an entire army of men there listening to this uncircumcised Philistine mock God day after day after day. Yet David, the young shepherd boy, was the only one who stepped up and took on this giant. His passion and love for God overruled his fear of death and defeat.

Is there a cause in your life that you are passionate about? Is there something you believe in so passionately that you are willing to risk it all for? How about your children? As a mother (and grandmother), I would do whatever necessary to save and protect my children. You don't want to face the wrath of a mama bear protecting her cubs or a mama human protecting her babies. That's the same way we should respond to someone dishonoring or defiling our God or the things of God. A Holy Passion should rise up within us and a fearless warrior should rise up out of us.

What are some of your passions that will cause you to take on the giants of your land? A few of mine are: Babies being murdered in the womb; children being hurt, abused or sold into sex trafficking; drug addicts overdosing and dying; women being abused by men; bully's picking on innocent people; school shootings; liars and fake news. I could go on and on. There's an old saying that says, "The only thing necessary for the triumph of evil is for good men (I'll add "or women") to do nothing." (By Edmund Burke in 1770)

This still stands true today and yes you can make a difference. Your voice can make a difference. Your vote can make a difference. Your prayer can make a difference. It starts with one.

When David asked that question, he was saying, "I would rather die with integrity and honor defending my God, then live with the shame of knowing that I cowered to a bully who mocked my God."

David's love for God was stronger than his fear of Goliath; his passion for God was stronger than his fear of death.

We need some giant-slayers. We need some Intercessor's who will pray through the night when called upon. We need some worshippers who will throw down their Kingly robes and worship passionately in the presence of God and unashamedly in the presence of man.

God is seeking out and searching for those who will not be intimidated by the voice of the enemy, but will stand strong in the face of fear. They have been forged in the fires of adversity and the refining fire of God has purged, cleansed and strengthened them for their journey.

It's time to take a stand and walk in the authority that God has given us. We have been passive, complacent and apathetic way too long. We have acquiesced to evil and wrong doings in the name of being a good Christian or turning the other cheek and Satan has taken full advantage of us. When dealing with a controlling, manipulating bully, you cannot remain passive and expect him to cower.

In Rev 2, The church was told to deal with Jezebel or it would not turn out well for them. We cannot tolerate this evil and expect it to just go away. Passivity won't slay giants. God expects us to deal with evil. Stand up against it and speak out.

Luk 10:19 (ESV) Behold, I have given you authority to tread on serpents and scorpions, and over all the power of the enemy, and nothing shall hurt you.

We must learn to fight the good fight of faith and run with endurance *the race that is set before us.*

You may have past regrets, let them go. You may have made mistakes and messed things up along your walk, learn from them and move forward. Let God use everything that you have been through in your life for His Glory!! He will!

Psa 27:4 One thing have I asked of the LORD, that will I seek after: that I may dwell in the house of the LORD all the days of my life, to gaze upon the beauty of the LORD and to inquire in his temple.

It is still God's desire to dwell with us....Heaven here on earth...

Exod. 29: 45 I have tabernacled in the midst of the sons of Israel, and have become their God.

It is my prayer that you are set on fire for God, that you experience the true fire of God that will refine you, purify you and burn up anything inside of you that is not of God. I pray that God will align you with Him first, then with others that He has destined you to be with. I pray that you will surrender yourselves fully to Him and follow Him in total obedience and fulfill your life calling. I pray that you will fall madly in Love with Jesus and your life will be changed forever. I pray that you will rise up in your God given authority as the governing body of the Church (Ekklesia) and become God's Warrior Bride.

May you surrender yourself under the mighty hand of God, place your heart in His hands and then by the power of the Holy Spirit, shift yourself first, then your family, your region and your nation! You can do this!

Jeremiah 51:20-21 (NLT) You are my battle-ax and sword," says the Lord. "With you I will shatter nations and destroy many kingdoms. With you I will shatter armies—

**We Are One Nation Under God! God Bless America and Let's all stand strong together and declare:
Tell the enemy we're coming and Heaven's coming with us!**

God bless you and may you become all that God created you to be!

Shelly J. Bishop

Hope you enjoyed this. If you have any questions or comments please
Feel free to email me at shellybishop4@gmail.com

Made in the USA
Columbia, SC
23 June 2023

18674612R00095